T0247706

Advance Praise for
# DARK TIDE

"The first memoir penned by a Bundy blood relative, *Dark Tide* is powerful and thought-provoking. Once fiercely loyal to a man she believed was falsely accused, Edna Cowell Martin shares her sense of betrayal as family pride turns to shame in this skillfully crafted journey. Ted Bundy was as close as a brother, and she trusted him implicitly until she witnessed bizarre behavior that forced her to face chilling revelations. Her secrets, held tightly for decades, are finally released in this unforgettable story."

> —Leslie Rule, author of *A Tangled Web—A Cyberstalker, a Deadly Obsession, and the Twisting Path to Justice*

"This is a fascinating first-hand story from a cousin who loved the most notorious serial killer in America. It is as fascinating as a true crime book can be, and equally incomprehensible."

> —David Crow, author of *The Pale-Faced Lie*

"A bone-chilling exploration of deception, delusion, and the personal trauma inflicted by the action of others, *Dark Tide* is a poignant and gut-wrenching journey across the minefields of perception, manipulation, and love. Suspenseful and absorbing from the start, with the drip, drip, drip of shocking hints, to the glass eventually overflowing, Martin carries us into the cognitive dissonance of the complex emotions, perceptions, and recollections experienced as she copes with the impact of her famous cousin's inexplicable acts on the family that thought they knew and loved him. A great, fascinating read. Highly recommended."

> — Leslie K. Simmons, author of *Red Clay, Running Waters*

# DARK TIDE

## GROWING UP WITH
## **TED BUNDY**

## EDNA COWELL MARTIN
## & MEGAN ATKINSON

PERMUTED
PRESS

A PERMUTED PRESS BOOK

Dark Tide:
Growing Up With Ted Bundy
© 2024 by ECMA Creative, LLC
All Rights Reserved

ISBN: 979-8-88845-060-4
ISBN (eBook): 979-8-88845-061-1

Cover art by Conroy Accord
Interior design and composition by Greg Johnson, Textbook Perfect

This is a work of nonfiction. All people, locations, events, and situations are portrayed to the best of the authors' memories.

PERMUTED
PRESS
**Permuted Press**
New York • Nashville
permutedpress.com

Published in the United States of America
2  3  4  5  6  7  8  9  10

*For Don, Anna, and John.*

*"You can accept a falling out that changes your plans,*
*but it's hard to accept a betrayal that changes your memories."*

—ROBERT BREAULT

*"Crocodiles are easy. They try to kill and eat you.*
*People are harder. Sometimes they pretend to be your friend first."*

—STEVE IRWIN

*This is a memoir, detailing events that happened half a century ago. We rely on memory as well as records, and while we've made accuracy a priority, any potential mistakes are unintended and our own.*

❋ ❋ ❋

*Please note, this book includes many real letters which contain errors. We've only corrected and noted the most serious errors in effort to stay true to the choices made in the originals.*

# Preface

For nearly fifty years I have avoided talking about Ted Bundy or acknowledging that he is my cousin. Whenever his name comes up, whether it is in a conversation, in print, or in the media, it feels like I can't catch my breath.

During the countdown to his execution, the media frenzy was overwhelming. Anyone who knew Ted was sought out for an interview. Incessant news reports about him blanketed the air. I lived in fear that the media would learn about me and track me down. Somehow, I was able to remain undetected and hidden from the insatiable press. In the midst of this chaotic time, I forged a friendship with a *Seattle Times* reporter who went out of his way to protect my identity. We shared a common bond of having both been deceived by Ted.

My brother and I were close to Ted. He and my brother were buddies and Ted treated me like his kid sister. Other than his mom and siblings, if anyone could "know" him, we felt for sure that we did. But, we didn't. Not at all.

I've asked myself over and over how I could have missed the signs. How could he be the cool Ted with me and my girlfriends and then turn around and abduct and violently murder girls who looked just like us with evident hatred and rage shortly afterward?

Some of my friends are still traumatized by having been exposed to Ted through me. One of my old roommates can't talk about him even to this day. So many people we know either directly or through friends knew one or more of the girls at the University of Washington in the early 1970s who was one of his victims. The wounds have not healed.

Why am I writing this book about Ted now? For so many years I've avoided facing up to the trauma he inflicted on all of us. I've protected my family and hidden my connection to Ted so we could live without the stain of his atrocities being somehow linked to us. We went on with our lives and I attempted to block him from my thoughts. Life kept us busy and full of challenges and adventures. But he always was lurking in the back of my mind. Social media won't let him fade away.

During the pandemic, my daughter and I went on long walks together. In the summer of 2021, on one of our walks, I told her that I didn't know why but I couldn't get Ted out of my mind and I needed to deal with it. This is when the idea of writing a book came up. A forbidden subject for so many years has finally found an outlet. It's a relief to tell my story.

—*Edna Cowell Martin*
2024

＊ ＊ ＊

"So what's your interest in my cousin Ted?"

Talk about an icebreaker. We were sitting on the back deck of Edna's daughter's house at the time, watching ferries crawl back and forth across Puget Sound against the silver Seattle skyline. The late summer day couldn't have been more pleasant, yet at that moment I found myself sweating.

How could I explain to this nice woman about the countless books on Ted Bundy that have taken turns on my bedside table, or about the hours upon hours of schlocky serial killer documentaries I've watched as a way to relax at the end of a hard day?

In any other context I'd be considered a big fan.

And I know I'm not the only one. The recent rise in popularity of true-crime has drawn hordes of us into the mainstream, giving us a community in which to air our morbid hobby.

But what, exactly, is the interest? I'd never put a fine point on it before, certainly not while staring into the eyes of a woman who'd actually lived it. What is our fascination with these true accounts of unimaginable horror?

As I fumbled for words and a coherent thought, maybe something about the evolutionary advantage of studying predators, Edna smiled at me. I could sense that she understood my dilemma much better than I did. After all, she'd seen others, floundering, in my shoes before. Then in an act I knew was kindness, she recast the line of inquiry—a progression in the conversation—and let me off the hook.

With that act and so many others since, I've come to realize that Edna herself represents the key to understanding at least my own interest in the genre. She's the humanity. While we can never fully understand men like Ted Bundy, Edna provides the context. Because we can't measure darkness without relating it to light.

But more importantly, the reverse is also true. Darkness reveals the mettle of a light. Over the course of writing this book, diving with Edna into the blackest corners of her story, I've come to see that any light, set amongst the deepest shadows, could so easily be swallowed up.

Or, as in Edna's case, it shines brighter.

—*Megan Atkinson*
2024

*Postcard from Unalaska, Alaska.*

# Prologue

## October, 1975

I had a phone call on the bridge.

The message was delivered by a man I didn't know but dimly recognized as a fellow crew member at Eastpoint Seafoods, from what department I couldn't say. He'd found me—unsurprisingly given our hours—on the production line, packaging freshly de-shelled king crab legs from the never-ending conveyor belt.

At first, I figured I'd heard him wrong—the constant whir of machinery left a ringing in our ears—or that he'd confused me with someone else. Since arriving at Dutch Harbor, in the Aleutian Islands that stretched like a kite tail off mainland Alaska, I'd already experienced a lot: harsh weather, unforgiving hours, feet that could never get warm in their steel-toed boots. Working at the conveyor belt, we stood on benches while ice-cold water sloshed underneath, sometimes balanced at unnerving angles when a delivery of fresh crab was dumped unevenly on the deck and caused the whole ship to list. I vividly remembered one night, not long after I'd arrived, when a drunken fistfight had erupted directly outside the one-room cabin on the beach I shared with several other girls. Afraid the brawlers could get inside, we'd dragged over our bunk beds to block the door and only knew the fight was finished when the banging and shuddering of the cabin walls finally ceased. Surely by now I was immune to surprises.

But this was unheard of.

From the other end of the belt, my friend Pamela watched our interaction with unease. She threw me a supportive look, but I didn't catch it.

Stunned, I removed my gloves and apron and, for the first time in the middle of a shift, stepped off the packing line.

\* \* \*

While escorted from the hold of the processing ship, I was told it was a "ship-to-shore" call, which felt even more ominous. I hadn't exactly made my coming to Alaska a secret, but neither had I announced it to the world. From the main deck, I had a good view of the small harbor surrounded by snow-capped mountains, the few buildings that made up the port town of Unalaska huddled near the onion-domed church as if for warmth or protection. I wondered who had tracked me down so far away from home. So far away from anything.

Climbing the stairs, I could see the windows of the bridge, silently presiding over its domain. I'd never been to the bridge. I didn't know anyone who had. Even at the top, I remember feeling the vibrations and thrumming of the machinery emanating from the bowels below. When the door to the bridge shut behind me, the air was quieter, but I could still feel it.

Inside was both more impressive and more beat-up than I'd expected. Monitors and controls lined the walls beneath the grimy windows, a backdrop for the ship's proud but rusted wheel. The ship's processing plant manager—a no-nonsense man with a Scandinavian accent— handed me a clunky phone and quickly demonstrated how to use it. As he stepped through a sliding door to give me privacy, I pushed a button on the receiver to answer. Curiosity battled with a heavy sense of apprehension.

It was my brother. The line was scratchy, but I knew his voice immediately, and the familiarity in this setting only increased my feeling of disorientation.

It took a couple tries to ask him what was going on. More radio than phone, only one person could transmit at a time, so conversation took some getting used to. Straining to listen, I understood John say he'd just received news.

Instantly my mind began to race. My parents were still young, as healthy as ever when I'd said goodbye to them the month before in September. Even my mother had been in reasonably high spirits considering the distance that would soon be between us. Surely this couldn't be about them. Could it?

John continued. Almost clinically, he explained that the police had made an arrest for a kidnapping in Utah, which they suspected to be connected to the serial killings that had gripped the Seattle area over the previous year.

I was interested, of course I was. Everyone in the city—especially we women in the U-District—had been following the reports and checking over our shoulders for so long our necks ached. But I was also confused why John was calling to pass on local news. Somewhere in my confusion, my gut quivered. From where I stood, I could see a crack in the sliding door where the plant manager had disappeared, and I began to wonder how much he could overhear.

When the line went silent, I didn't know if our connection was lost or if it was something else. I had never known my brother to be emotional, but a fragile tone in his voice was scaring me. Finally, the speaker crackled again.

"It's Ted," he said.

# Letter from Ted to Edna

*Written from prison after Edna reached out to Ted to ask what he thought of Ann Rule's recently published book about him,*
The Stranger Beside Me.

*Transcription of entire letter.*

September 9, 1980

Dear Edna,

What a totally unexpected present your recent letter was. I honestly cannot put into words the delight I experienced upon receiving and reading your letter. I want to return a letter to you immediately since I have found that the longer I wait to respond to a letter, the less likely I am to respond at all.

Until recently I generally confined my correspondence to my wife. She, in turn, would relay messages as needed. I never have been very fond of letter writing anyway. However, this lazy-man's approach did not lessen my nagging sense of discomfort that I was neglecting to keep in touch with people I care about. So I have begun a [sic] write a couple non-spousal notes each week. It's good responsibility therapy, also.

Yes, it has been nearly five years since we last saw each other in person. But since my sense of time has been warped, five years or five months are spans of time, the difference between which I find hard to appreciate. My life, in the idea of time, is divided into two eras. B.C. (Before court/cops) and A.D (After Damnation). One life ended and another began once I began living in prison. When I look at the part of my life which took place before 1975, I might very well be looking at an existence as one might view a prior incarnation.

\* \* \*

Thanks for all the news about yourself and family. I was not aware of your dad's heart attack. How distressing. Please convey to him my belated relief that his recovery has been complete.

$435 dollars a month rent for a cottage north of Lake City Way?! You're damn right things have changed since I was in Seattle. (So much has changed, it seems I don't find it hard to imagine that free people live in a different world than I live in now or back when I was a free person.)

4

# Prologue

Your rent is close to double what it would have been five years ago. I am familiar with the area across from the 7-11. Déjà vu, do you suppose?

Your parents told me about your work when I saw them last in Tallahassee. You seem to have mixed emotions about it. I sense that you are finding some rewards. I know firsthand of the conflicts a young woman, wife and mother feels in such a position.

\* \* \*

The man who collects the mail will be by shortly, so be prepared for an abrupt ending. I will write again soon, and attempt to answer your questions about my life here. It will take some time to put into words the way things are and the way I am.

The long and short of it, and the irony are that I am in better shape mentally and physically than I can ever remember being in before. This may be a delusion. I have been happier. But perhaps that was a delusion. The problem is that I find it hard to make comparisons between two alien environments. More later, though.

\* \* \*

If you have $14.95 to throw away on badly written fiction (that's a small amount of truth mixed with a large amount of fiction), then buy Ann Rule's book. I would not ever tell someone not to read something. In this case, I might not be the best judge. I can offer my undeniably informed opinion.

The half-truths, misrepresentations and outright fictionalizations Rule, and the others as well, engages in puzzle me....

The man cometh

Love you.

Give my love to all.

Thanks for the wonderful letter.

Ted

*Young Ted (right) with Edna's mother and brother (left).*

# One of the Family

In 1950, my first cousin Louise and her four-year-old son, Ted—"Teddy" as he was known then—left Philadelphia to move to Tacoma and live with my family. By the time I was born the following year, my life would be forever intertwined with Ted Bundy's.

*  *  *

It was my father—John R. Cowell—who had the idea for Louise to relocate all the way across the country. She'd given birth to Ted out of wedlock, and back in the 1940s, that had made life difficult for the young mother still residing in the community where she'd grown up. My dad felt a change of scenery could give her a fresh start, a real chance at a new life, and with my mother's blessing he invited Louise and her baby boy into our small family home.

Though technically his niece, Louise was only a few years younger than my dad, who, as the last of seven kids, was twenty years younger than his oldest sibling and Louise's father, Sam Cowell. But the label of their relationship didn't matter to my father. She was family, period. And that went for Ted as well.

As his children, we inherited the sentiment. Though in reality, Louise was my first cousin, I always referred to her son as "my cousin Ted." But in truth I thought of him more like another brother, or, as we grew up together, simply my friend.

*  *  *

7

It was fall when Louise packed up Ted and moved to Tacoma. In letters to our Aunt Ginny—letters that came into my possession after the passing of my parents—she expressed a desire to wait through the summer and help her dad, a landscaper in Philadelphia, during his busy season. According to Louise, she didn't want to leave him stranded.

Much has been made regarding Louise's relationship with her father and if Sam could possibly be Ted's real dad. I don't believe this to be the case. I can say with certainty that I never saw nor heard murmur of anything untoward in that respect. I understand that my uncle Sam could be a difficult man at times, though I can't speak about this from any personal experience as he was nothing but kind to me in all of our meetings. Louise's letters seem to show she had real affection for him.

Yet, I also admit that even inside a family, it's difficult to know what goes on behind closed doors. I suppose the rest of my story proves that point.

Louise and Ted lived with my parents and older brother for the better part of a year until Louise found a house nearby in Tacoma. Despite Ted's young age, I believe in those months under my family's roof, my father established himself as a significant male figure to Ted. Since Louise firmly refused to name the man who'd fathered him, Ted recognized a hole where a father figure should have been, and I know it always bothered him.

The following year in 1951—which was also the year that I was born—Louise met and married Johnnie Bundy, a kind, hardworking cook in the kitchen at the Madigan Army Medical Center, who adopted Ted and gave him his last name. Louise and Johnnie went on to have four children of their own, and though they all shared the Bundy moniker, even to my young eyes, I could see that Ted kept himself slightly apart. He was a little older, so age likely factored in, but I believe more lay at the core.

Ted had visions of a grand life, and he liked to elevate himself as special. He exhibited an early cleverness, and Louise's continual remarks that he was special and full of potential only nurtured Ted's position. It seemed important to him, even as a young boy, to pose himself as someone destined for big things.

I wonder sometimes if my family had something to do with that.

* * *

Both college educated, my mother and father had served as officers in the military during World War II. My mother—Eleanor Gellert—was promoted to lieutenant as a communication officer in the navy, where she served in the first class of WAVES (Women Accepted for Volunteer Emergency Service). There she managed a team of over a hundred people who worked to decode enemy transmissions, even uncovering a plot for a German submarine to enter Chesapeake Bay. Their efforts prevented that from happening.

My mother complained about having to carry a gun. Hailing from Philadelphia high society, she was an elegant lady, always impeccably dressed, and she didn't think the gun went with her uniform. "It broke up the lines," she'd say when she told us stories of her past.

Meanwhile, my dad served as a lieutenant in the army, where he played a portable field organ for Sunday services. Before his unit was set to be deployed, he took part in a training exercise that put him on a boat crossing the Potomac River with live artillery and mortar fire going off all around. Somehow the timing went awry, and an explosive detonated right underneath the boat with my father on board. One of his fellow soldiers was killed on the spot. My dad, though severely wounded, survived.

He always said the training accident saved his life. Shortly after he was hospitalized, his army unit was sent to Guadalcanal to fight in

*John "Jack" Cowell and Eleanor Gellert in uniform.*

Operation Watchtower, the first major land offensive by allied forces against the Empire of Japan. Many of the guys in his unit never made it home.

My dad chose to spend his rehabilitation period at the family home of his high school sweetheart—my mother—in Meadowbrook, right outside of Philadelphia. His brushes with death had put him in mind of what he really wanted in life. At the end of the six weeks, he proposed.

They were married in 1943, in the middle of the war. In accordance with protocol, Dad wore his dress uniform. Mom got special permission from the Navy to wear a wedding dress. No gun.

* * *

My father was a gifted musician. Even from his childhood, which he spent playing the pipe organ at church and sneaking off to Harlem to visit jazz clubs, he'd known he wanted to make music his life's pursuit. After the war—after studying under Paul Hindemith at Yale where my brother, John Jr., was born—he and my mother packed up their Buick and moved to Tacoma where he began teaching, composing, and building his career as a concert pianist.

They'd set their sights on the Seattle area largely because that's where my mother's parents had recently relocated, having uprooted from Philadelphia when her father took the post as head of Seattle Gas Company. As a new mother herself, my mom missed them terribly. Over the years, more and more of her family followed suit, migrating to the Pacific Northwest and building a strong support system of Gellerts.

But for Louise and Ted, they'd left the rest of the Cowells behind in Philadelphia. Until Louise married, we were their only family in the west and their only link to her branches on the family tree.

This, I believe, brought our families closer together.

* * *

Ted adored my father, maybe even idolized him. I could hardly blame him. I did, too.

I knew that Jack Cowell wasn't like most dads. Somehow, I think I still took it for granted, in that "aw shucks, Dad" everyday kind of way.

He was a force of nature, my dad, living each day to the brim. With his naturally artistic temperament, he saw any challenge or fork in the road as an opportunity for fun, for play, for creation. And he was always up to something, whether composing a new ballet or learning to water ski or arranging a concert for kids. The doorbell would ring nonstop with other artist friends stopping by to visit and play music.

Our home was filled with music.

On the rare occasions that I found his piano unattended, I'd eagerly sit down and plunk out keys. If I hit a wrong note, I'd hear my dad's exasperated voice yell from somewhere outside: "B flat!"

When he prepared for a concert, he'd practice the difficult parts so many times, I'd lie awake in bed and count, once all the way to two-hundred and fifty. It wasn't until he moved on to the next measure that I could finally fall asleep.

On a cross-country trip back to the Northeast, I remember sitting in the audience with him as we attended a performance by the Philadelphia Symphony conducted by Eugene Ormandy, a former mentor of my father's. As the featured piano soloist played, I saw tears streaming down Dad's cheeks, and I grew distressed. But as the performance continued, somehow I came to understand. The tears were joy and admiration. My father was so full of life, sometimes it leaked out.

✳ ✳ ✳

While Ted and the Bundys further settled in Tacoma, our families lived within ten minutes of each other, and our lives were frequently overlapping. Things changed, however, as my father's career began to take off in earnest.

Beginning when I was six years old, much of my early childhood was spent traveling the world as my father toured. We'd stay in hotels for months at a time while my dad performed his own concerts or as a soloist with grand symphonies. I remember loving the Eloise books because she lived in a hotel. I could relate.

In 1959, we spent several months in New York while my father played at Town Hall on Forty-Third Street, one of the premier concert venues in the city. At that time, my parents were particularly excited to see the new play *West Side Story*, since the music had been written by my father's good friend from his Philadelphia Conservatory and Tanglewood days, Leonard Bernstein.

With its mechanized Times Square billboards and the Horn & Hardart automat cafeteria, I found the city to be a magical place, though one of my most vivid memories of it occurred when a man pushed aside my mother and me to poach the taxi we'd hailed. It was a cold, winter day, and I remember the man's arm as it thrust in front of us, pushing us out of the way, so he could slide into the warm interior first.

"Huh!" my mother said, which was about the foulest thing I ever heard her say.

From New York, we set sail on a ship to Europe. As a child, I made this trip twice for a total of four transatlantic crossings. I can still remember the explosions of confetti as we pushed off from the pier, and we waved to my mother's brother and his family who had come to see us off. Flutes of champagne were passed amongst the adults, and I watched my parents toast in celebration as we passed right by the Statue of Liberty and sailed out to sea.

* * *

In Europe, my father played in Paris, Lisbon, Vienna, Athens...more exotic locations than my young mind could comprehend. After every concert, a gala would be thrown in his honor. With my stylish mother at his side, dressed—as usual—in pearls and fur, they made a perfect couple, wined and dined by the affluent and elite of the music world.

While teaching in Tacoma, my father had been on the music faculty at the College of Puget Sound and became great friends with Manuel Rosenthal, the composer in residence on sabbatical from his home of Paris. Mr. Rosenthal had been Ravel's third and final student. During his tenure as the music director of the Seattle Symphony, Mr. Rosenthal invited my father to play as a featured piano soloist on many occasions. After he returned home, Manuel Rosenthal accepted the post of conductor for the Paris Radio Symphony, and it was on his invitation that our family spent several years, off and on, living in Paris.

Our first visit—in 1959—lasted about six months. We rented a villa on the outskirts of the city in a little village called Wissou that came with a studio containing a grand piano for my father.

Above the double doors to the studio hung a stuffed albatross. I remember staring up at it. To my young eyes, the bird seemed monstrously huge with its ten-foot wingspan. I'd been told that it was bad luck to kill an albatross, and standing below it, I worried it could be a bad omen.

I learned, then, how to hold two conflicting emotions in my heart simultaneously. I felt sorry for the creature. But I was also scared of it.

❊ ❊ ❊

Over the wall of the house next door, we'd occasionally hear the voices of British nannies, and I quickly learned the family residing there had a young daughter named Elizabet. Though I was a few years older, I loved playing with Elizabet, whom I thought very cute, and her nannies doted on me and told me how much they loved to listen over the wall when my father practiced in his studio.

I later learned that Elizabet was a princess, part of the von Habsburg family that had escaped Austria and the Nazis during World War II. It was probably a decade later when my mother and I saw a photo of her, Princess Elizabet, in *Paris Match* magazine, which my mother subscribed to for years. At the time, I had no idea I was playing with royalty, and I'm not sure it would have mattered if I did.

We returned to Paris a couple of years later, and John and I enrolled at the English School of Paris, which had many kids from prestigious families as students. One of my best friends was the son of the American Ambassador to Paris. I didn't care in the slightest who his dad was. I just thought he was nice.

I remember getting invited to his birthday party. My mother made sure to put me in my best dress before taking me to the apartment building where my friend lived, located in one of the toniest quarters of Paris. When I knocked on the door, a maid answered and took my coat, welcoming me inside to a vast, ornate flat. I remember being very intimidated. Aside from my friend, I didn't know anyone else there, and I counted the minutes until I could leave.

But this was simply the world exposed to us by my parents from a young age. My brother and I didn't know to be impressed or reverent about our experiences, much less snobby. To us, this was ordinary life, as regular as our days catching sand crabs in Puget Sound, and we'd chatter on and on, telling the stories at home when our cousins came to visit.

*Edna's family in promotional photo for newspaper.*

Ted, in particular, seemed interested in our accounts of the upper crust. I don't know how much I really understood then, but I got the impression he found something in those stories that he wanted for himself. He wouldn't settle for a small life.

Ted Bundy was going to be somebody.

# Letters from Louise to Aunt Ginny
# (Sister of Edna's Father)

*Transcriptions of entire letters.*

May 3, 1950

Dear Aunt Ginny:

Your letter came today and mere words can't express my feelings when I read it. I think I am certainly the most fortunate girl in this world to have such a loving and thoughtful person as you for an Aunt. In fact, all my Daddy's family have been so wonderful to me since they learned of my troubles that I am completely overwhelmed.

I have been considering this move ever since Jack and Eleanor first extended the invitation several years ago. I feel it will be the best thing for Teddy and also for me. I decided this some time ago, but various things have delayed my going. First of all, I've been reluctant to leave daddy too suddenly because he depends on me so much for helping him with the business. (Too bad he didn't have a son. But sons don't often follow their father's business either, do they?) He knows now, however, that I want to get away and is trying to make plans accordingly. My Daddy's such a darling and has worked so hard all his life, it just doesn't seem fair to leave him in the lurch at this critical time when his business is just beginning to take hold.

My plan, then, is to finish helping him this season and make the trip early Sept. That's still a nice time to travel and will give me time to get things ready.

Your offer of financial help is very gratefully accepted. I was wondering just how I would make ends meet. I did have some money of my own but have had to use it for various things. Fifty dollars of it went to the Legal Aid Society for helping me change Teddy's last name. My own name, they told me, did not need to be changed in court. I can, legally, just assume another last name. The procedure about Teddy's name hasn't gone thru yet because the lawyer is trying to save me the money. He thinks there's a possibility of doing it without costing me fifty dollars. So I'm waiting to hear from him on that. It's too long and complicated to explain here. Next time I see you perhaps it will be straightened out and I can tell you all about it.

Daddy would like to help me financially, and probably will a little, but all his money is tied up in the business and I'd rather accept as little from him as possible.

I think you are wonderful to be willing to give up your trip West in order to help me. I am really humble in the face of such love and unselfishness. And, I would certainly be willing to pay it all back in time, if you wanted me to. However, if as you say in your letter, you would rather give me part and then lend me a little to get started, that would be wonderful. I am certainly not at all hesitant about accepting your offer, am I? Well frankly, I do need such help very much and don't quite see how I'd manage without it. Your letter came at a time when my morale really needed a boost and succeeded in doing just that. A person can only do so much by herself, you know and then once in a while has to look to others for help. I've tried to keep as much of my burden on my own shoulders as possible, but it's a wonderful help to have others share it with me occasionally. Otherwise, I'd get very weary.

I'll be tied up with work for the next 3 or 4 weeks, but perhaps after that we could get together and talk things over.

Teddy's getting to be quite a big boy already. He's started investigating the neighborhood now and I spend half my time searching for him, it seems. The fact that he is old enough (and wise enough) to be doing that is all the more reason for us to be "up and away" from here.

Thanks so very much for being so generous and thoughtful. Hope we'll be seeing you soon.

Love,

Louise


Oct. 3rd

Dear Aunt Ginny:

It seems so hard for us to get together or even to find a good time to talk on the phone, that I thought I'd write to you. Maybe I can convey my thoughts better that way, anyhow. I just finished writing to Aunt Helen, too, and want to put the same things into this letter as I did in hers.

Both Aunt Helen and I had a telegram from Jack this past weekend. Mine said:

"Come as our niece, everything cleared. Can you come the 9th?"

(That was the date I had previously said I would arrive.) The one to Aunt Helen was mainly to inform her of the one he had sent me. It gave me some encouragement. At least there was one problem that was fairly well solved. I have not received a letter from him explaining how they manage to get "everything cleared," but don't suppose he would have sent the telegram if it were not. They know I have changed my name to Nelson and will have to come as that and now say it's all right to be their niece, so I'm assuming or hoping that they hadn't told people too much and could add the "niece" part without anything seeming amiss.

On the strength of that and coupled with a few other things I have decided to go next week on Tuesday, the 10th, arriving there on the 16th.

The other reasons for my decision are these:

Audy says that she and Shorty will not be in Seattle after the 25th of Oct. They are being transferred to another base about a hundred miles distant. If I don't go quickly, then, I won't even get to see her, not to mention her helping me with finding a place to live or taking care of Teddy.

Then, too, the cold weather will be setting in soon in those states through which I must travel. I'd rather not travel in cold weather, nor do I want to wait until next Spring.

So, this is what I would like to do:

Go to Jack & Eleanor's when I first arrive there, but with no more intention of staying longer than I would if I got temporary lodging at the Y.W.

As I said to Aunt Helen there are several reasons why I would like to go there first. One concerns Teddy. I have told him where we are going, all about John, etc. He's looking forward to it. If, instead we went to the "Y" where he would of necessity be more confined, have no children to play with; in short not do what I said we were going to do, I don't think the effect would be good on him. As for myself, I would feel much better and enjoy the trip more if I know exactly where I am going to live for the first few weeks. It's hard enough to be making this break without having the added burden of arriving in a strange city with no place to go except a hotel or the like with no one around I know or can talk to. I do want to be on my own, but not quite so abruptly as that.

I expect to stay at Jack's only the shortest possible time and to immediately start looking for a Day Nursery, job, and apartment. Meanwhile I want to pay my way while living at Jack's, of course.

17

It will be so much nicer after a day's searching to come back to a home where there's someone I know and can talk to. It will be an incentive to me, really. It will be understood from the first that we won't stay long so neither of us will become dependent on the other for anything. So far as I'm concerned, it seems the best thing to do, and I hope you understand how I feel. I can assure you it will only be very temporary and I'll be off on my own before you know it.

Since I am going, the matter of finances needs to be settled. I figure that the trip will cost between $125 and $130. That's carfare, hotel rooms, and food. I have about $75 of that, Daddy having given me most of it. As I told you I had to spend almost all I had saved on various other things. Daddy would like to give me more, but is hard pressed at the time. He doesn't like me to have to borrow, but if I'll be sure to pay it back when I'm able, it will be all right. In other words, before I can buy my ticket, I'll have to borrow some from you. I'd like to get my ticket by Saturday, at least. As to what else you can lend me, I'll leave that up to you. Or, putting it very bluntly, I need about $50 towards the trip out there and whatever you can spare me to live on for from 2 to 4 weeks.

I hope you don't mind my writing this way, but to me it seemed the quickest and best way to tell you what I want to do.

Perhaps you could give me a call when you receive this and let me know what you think and how the finances can be arranged.

I deeply appreciate your concern and thoughtfulness in all this trouble of mine, believe me: I'll never be able to thank you enough.

Love,

Louise

*Front*

Feb 6, 1959

Dear Grandad:

I guess I haven't thanked you for the presents you sent me. Thank you for the scout knife, signal flags, master reels, Monopoly set.

My scout knife came in handy today when we took the five mile hike for second class. I cooked a meal of fried potato, hamburgers, hot chocolate, and a couple of apples. My hamburger caught fire when I put it in the fire to cook faster, and when I went to shake the salt the cap fell off and all the salt fell into my potato while they were cooking. It all tasted good anyway.

We'll be having a board of review and I'm going to make my second class then, I hope.

If we come back there this summer I hope I'll be on my way to first class and be started on some merit badges.

I guess I have to close for now. Say hello to everybody for me. Hope everybody is feeling well.

Your Grandson
Ted

*Back*

Transcription of Louise's note on back: "P.S. He did get his second class award. We had a very nice Parent's Night last week with a Pot-Luck [sic] supper followed by a Court of Honor when the awards were presented. Please forgive Ted for not writing more. He has so much to do and letter writing is rather a chore for him.

The Scout troop is going on our overnight camping trip this weekend— the 21st and 22nd. Hope the weather dries off. It has been very wet and chilly this week."

*Ted stands with Edna's family for a photo. Left to right: Edna (on horse), John, Ted, Jack, Edna's friend, Margie (on horse), Eleanor. Louise and Johnnie Bundy pose on the right with their children.*

# Longbranch

When we weren't traveling, home still meant Washington, which also meant the Bundys.

Though my parents had sold our home in Tacoma when we began spending extended periods away, they retained a small beach cabin on the Key Peninsula in a remote town called Longbranch. This became our homebase. It was here where we'd return from our travels, and here where the Bundys would come to visit.

When my parents first bought it in the mid-fifties, the cabin was nothing but a rundown shack, inhabitable only to the legions of spiders living inside. But with three acres of land and four-hundred feet of waterfront, they saw the diamond in the rough and quickly set out to bring it back to life.

To all of us, the cabin represented paradise. Even our cat, Fluff, would meow excitedly whenever we'd turn down the familiar road leading to the property. Considering that the Bundys bought a lake cabin of their own years later, I believe they loved these escapes from the city as much as we did.

\* \* \*

One summer when I was about twelve or thirteen, the Bundys came to visit. I remember I wore my striped T-shirt for the occasion, which I'd begged my mom to purchase because it reminded me of those worn by the Beach Boys in recent promotional photos I'd seen.

I remember the Bundys pulling up in their Nash Rambler station wagon. No sooner had it parked than the four younger kids tumbled out, bouncing with excitement for a day of play.

Ted was the last of the kids to get out. By then he must have been seventeen or eighteen, and the age difference to his siblings appeared more pronounced. Whereas the kids squirmed and wiggled, he stood up straight and carried himself with an air of budding maturity.

As I ran up from the beach, Ted graciously greeted me. When he asked me how I was doing, Ted always looked me in the eye, and I felt he was truly paying attention. It didn't matter what he asked—"What are you up to?" "How do you like school?"—the way he asked was most important.

Kids get a lot of questions about themselves, but they're smart enough to know when someone's actually interested. Ted always gave his full attention and interest. He knew how to make a person feel special. I loved him for that.

Later on, he learned he could use this skill to his terrible advantage.

* * *

That day, we did a little bit of everything.

With the beach, the forest, and the water at our disposal, we never ran out of things to do when the Bundys came to visit. We'd explore the shore and play badminton. I'd take turns shuttling the kids out on boats or around on horses borrowed from neighbors for the day. We'd find old apple trees still producing fruit and eat them straight off the branches. Sometimes we'd go up to the attic to scare ourselves with made-up tales about the ghost of Whiskey Pete Olsen, our nickname for a previous owner of the property.

On those beach days with the Bundys, Ted had as much fun as any of us, though I don't remember him being particularly adventurous. While I looked for any excuse to water ski—a passion I shared with my dad—and John loved climbing trees, Ted generally preferred to stay earthbound. I got the sense that he didn't like relinquishing his sense of control.

Everyone's favorite event was low tide, when we could run far out onto the sand and find tidepools full of weird, delightful creatures. John and I would show the others how to catch sand crabs, and Ted would make me laugh as he let them crawl over his palm before letting them go.

Louise would usually bring dishes of food for a picnic, and my mom would often make chowders or stews from clams or oysters we harvested from our beach. We'd all gather outside to eat while the adults talked. Ted had begun participating in the discussion more, and he sought out my father, asking him questions on topics that seemed boring to me at the time. But even still, there was something distinctly comforting in their grown-up din, and I'd lean my head on my father's shoulder, feeling the vibrations of his voice as I watched the boats come in and out of the bay.

These were idyllic days, golden-hued and carefree, and Ted was a big part of them. I really got the sense that he loved my family, and we loved him.

That is, looking back, what makes it all so difficult.

\* \* \*

At some point that day, we gathered for a family picture, wrangling a neighbor kid to take it so we could get everyone in frame.

As we all faced the camera and waited for the click, from the corner of my eye I saw Ted dislodge himself from his position amongst the Bundys and slide over to stand with my family on the opposite side of the group.

When the camera snapped, Ted stood with John and me by my parents.

Even at the time, I thought that was strange.

\* \* \*

Because Ted and John were the same age, they spent a lot of time together and became very close friends. All growing up, when our families got together, the two older boys would often go to John's room to listen to music, or take a boat into the bay, or find new trails to hike through the forest—usually with Fluff stalking behind.

Though they were teenage boys, John says he and Ted never got up to anything abnormal or unseemly when they were together, and I believe him. They never looked at pornography, violent or otherwise, though

John does remember seeing Ted reading pulpy detective novels, the kind with vaguely smutty art on the covers, usually featuring a provocative-ly-dressed woman in a vulnerable position with a man looming above, holding a gun. At the time, John recalls feeling they were probably too young for such reading material though he didn't say anything about it.

John remembers visiting Ted at his house in Tacoma when they were teenagers, particularly Ted's bedroom, which John described as "bleak." John was taken aback that there were no decorations, no knickknacks, and not a thing on the walls. Whereas John's bedroom was filled with posters, artwork, and implements of his many hobbies, Ted's showed no sign of self-expression. John didn't know if that was Ted's personal choice or a house rule. He simply didn't know what to make of it.

* * *

I didn't really become aware that my brother was different until later. He was just my brilliant older brother—sure, a little goofy, but all boys seemed goofy to me. These days, we understand he'd have been diag-nosed as being mildly on the spectrum, or spectrum adjacent.

John's fascination with most any topic knew no limits. He was simply inexhaustible when it came to learning—I've never known anyone to have such a hunger. When his nose wasn't buried in a book, I remember him building with his erector set, constructing the most impressive contraptions from what looked to me like random, metal pieces.

While traveling, when we weren't stationed in one place long enough to enroll in English schools, our education fell to my mother, who used the Calvert Education correspondence school. For both John and me, she was the best teacher. My mother personalized our studies, and she had the entirety of Europe to use as a textbook. When learning about an event from history, we could actually travel to the site where it had happened. I was always thrilled by the excursions, but John especially lapped it up, his brain practically humming as he absorbed every detail.

But at home in Washington, John was an absolute nuisance at school. The curriculum left him so bored that he acted up in class, wiggling underneath the desks and causing disruptions. His teachers had no idea what to do with him, and instead of channeling their efforts into helping this curious, energetic kid, they threw up their hands and said there must be something wrong with him. They'd call my mother in for conferences and blame her for making their lives miserable. John was a problem, they said. He needed to have his head examined.

Because John struggled so much in the local junior high school, my parents finally made the decision to put him in private school, one with better discipline and a curriculum more suited to his needs. They never could have afforded to do this on my father's salary alone, but my mother's parents helped. They, too, wanted the best chance for their grandson.

So, for a year in junior high, John enrolled in a private boarding school in Victoria, Canada. I loved to go visit since we'd stay at the Empress Hotel, which I thought looked like a castle, and we'd take high tea in the lounge in the afternoons.

John did well at that school, and it proved to my parents that he required something beyond what our local public education could offer. The following year, when my father started his doctorate program at the University of Washington, and we settled more permanently in Seattle, John was placed in Lakeside, a private high school where he could take college courses through the university. He flourished.

Since they were such good friends, I have to think my brother's intelligence and private education marked another notch for Ted to measure himself. I know he compared himself to John. Comments he made in later years—comments for which I'll never forgive him—showed that to be the case.

# Letter from Ted to Edna

*Written from prison, after receiving no response to his
previous letter dated 9/9/1980.*

*Transcription of entire letter.*

December 11, 1980

Dear Edna,

How long has it been since we exchanged letters? (I hope you received
the letter I sent in return to your last letter.) Too long.

I hope husband, child and work are doing well, still. When you can pin
John down tell him for me to stop neglecting me or I'll let the air out of
his tires. He owes me a hamburger and fries but an apologetic note will
do just fine to square accounts.

I'm in unusually good shape. The Christmas season invariably has this
effect on me, and the spirit of the season even finds its way in here. I
stretch a lot, don't eat meats or sweets, stopped smoking (again) and
am learning Spanish from a Cuban and Columbian [sic] who live just
down the street from me. They call me El Abogado (the lawyer) by the
way, which is an improvement over what my Chicano friends used to call
me, Conejo (rabbit).

Let me know what's up and what isn't. My love to you this Christmas,

Ted B

*Pergola at Far-A-Way.*

# Far-A-Way

A short walk up the beach from our cabin on Filucy Bay, at the end of our tiny peninsula, sat a grand estate called Far-A-Way. Our little cabin would be considered rustic. Far-A-Way was something else entirely.

Set on six acres, the estate perched on a promontory overlooking Puget Sound with a commanding view of the bay and surrounding islands. The property had over a thousand feet of waterfront with a sprawling mansion and enormous dock—complete with a boatlift—offering plenty of space for numerous yachts to tie up.

Far-A-Way constituted an important part of the DNA of Long-branch, and I remember bringing Ted there when he visited. I can still picture him walking into the lodge-like front room, looking around in awe at the caribou head presiding atop the artisan river rock fireplace and other animals mounted on the surrounding walls—a moose and deer head, ducks, and wild turkeys. When the Bundys were visiting, Ted would always perk up with interest whenever we had stories to share about Far-A-Way. And there were many stories about Far-A-Way.

* * *

When my family first purchased our cabin, we understood it had once been part of the Far-A-Way estate. At that time, the main property was abandoned and quite dilapidated, and I remember exploring the house with my family.

Carefully we stepped through the spacious rooms with soaring ceilings. It was obvious that the mansion had been uninhabited for a long time. What furniture remained had been piled into corners, everything in tatters. As our footsteps echoed through the space, it was as if we could hear ghosts whispering to us from the past. What had happened here, and why had it been abandoned?

We learned that it had been built in 1915 by Josephine and Frank McDermott, of the *Bon Marché* department store dynasty. The couple had loved hosting lavish, *Gatsby*-esque parties at the estate, shuttling in friends and store employees via steamboat across the bay and from points far and wide on Puget Sound. Longbranch locals were hired to cook and chop firewood, and occasionally at the parties, one would spot a Hollywood starlet or even—rumor had it—a United States president.

A few years after we bought our cabin, Far-A-Way was purchased by a new family and completely restored. I was about seven at the time, and I remember one morning I concocted a plan. Armed with a basket of fresh-picked blackberries, I waved goodbye to my parents and set off on foot to Far-A-Way.

Limiting myself to eating only a few berries along the way, I soon saw a figure up ahead on a ladder, and I recognized the man as our new neighbor, Mr. Palmer. As I watched, he hung a sign at the entrance of Far-A-Way's dramatic pergola.

*Far-A-Way*, the sign said.
*Come oft to the house of thy friends*
*Lest weeds grow in thy path.*

I waited patiently for Mr. Palmer to finish hanging the sign, then I cleared my throat and presented him with the blackberries.

"Do any kids live here?" I asked, betraying my mission's true objective. I was dying for some local playmates.

Mr. Palmer stepped down from the ladder. At six feet four inches, he towered over me, but he was kind-looking with dark hair and a trimmed mustache, the latter of which twitched as he smiled.

He told me he had a few grandchildren he expected to visit soon, and I should come by to play when they arrived. As I tried to contain my excitement, he then asked me if I'd bring the blackberries to his wife at the house.

In graphic detail, I remember stepping down the cobbled walk of the two-hundred-foot-long pergola, pausing to admire the hanging baskets of begonias and fuchsias and trying the porch swings situated in several spots along the way. I gazed up at the bell atop the gazebo and found a wishing well constructed from river rock. I felt as if I'd entered through the gates of a fairy tale.

When I reached the house, a beautiful woman with her blond hair in a French twist greeted me and accepted my gift with such enthusiasm, the fairy tale was complete.

"Come oft to the house of thy friends," the sign had said.

For the next twenty-five years, I'd do just that.

\* \* \*

My mission hadn't been in vain. The Palmers' granddaughter, Margie, came to visit not long after, and we quickly became inseparable. In fact, she remains one of my best friends to this day, both of us now in our seventies.

Margie and her younger siblings would often spend their summers visiting their grandparents at Far-A-Way, so I, in turn, often spent much of my summers at Far-A-Way. Margie and I did everything together, from horseback riding to treasure hunts to sleeping in tents, toting along flashlights, snacks, and comic books. She and I probably walked every inch of that shore, collecting shells and mussels. At twelve, my parents trusted me to pilot our eighteen-foot speedboat myself—a freedom and privilege I was determined to honor by adhering to all safety protocols drilled in by my father—and Margie and I enjoyed exploring the bay and gathering up our friends for water-skiing excursions.

The Palmers' son, Clarke, was six and a half years older than me and one of the most naturally sociable people I've ever met. Margie and I had the perfect vantage point to observe his teenage activities. It seemed to us that Clarke had an endless stream of girlfriends, and we loved watching as they came to the house, comparing them and picking our favorites. I'm sure we must have been annoying, but Clarke never made us feel that way.

All the kids around the bay nurtured a good-humored prank war for years. It was harmless fun really, though Margie and I probably took it too far the day we painted Clarke's friend's station wagon with peace signs.

The stunt might have been a decent joke—except we used house paint. Not satisfied to go halfway, we completely covered all the windows with the paint before running away, giggling our asses off.

Years later, I learned they spent hours scraping paint off those windows, but there was little to be done to salvage the vehicle. I found out that Clarke bought his friend a "new" beater car as a result. It still makes my stomach drop when I think of it.

＊ ＊ ＊

On one of his visits to Longbranch, Ted found himself in the midst of the prank war.

It was a hot summer afternoon, and while I ran around with the younger Bundy kids, John and Ted took our blunt-nosed rowboat out into the bay in front of our house. John, having more experience, did most of the rowing while Ted sat back and enjoyed the ride.

From behind, they heard the roar of an engine, and they turned to see a boat approaching, coming in close and fast. John recognized the boat, a twenty-eight-foot Fairliner, as belonging to the Palmers. And sure enough, Clarke stood at the helm, towing another friend from across the bay, expertly slalom skiing behind.

This was not a small boat, and it put out a significant wake. As they passed, the girl on the ski leaned over and cut back, launching a giant wall of spray that drenched Ted and John in the pram, immediately followed by the Fairliner's huge wake, which sent them rocking.

John held tight to the sides and laughed, complimented by the attention from a girl and already beginning to scheme how he'd get them back. But Ted had a much different reaction.

He was furious, so over-the-top enraged that it left a lasting impression on John, he told me later. What John found especially disturbing, he said, was that he'd never seen Ted react like that before.

On the boat, John tried to calm Ted down by explaining that they were friends, and we always pulled pranks on one another. It was all good fun.

But Ted didn't care. He'd been the butt of a joke. He didn't like that at all.

＊ ＊ ＊

In the true spirit of Far-A-Way, the new owners picked up the tradition of hosting parties right where the McDermotts left off. These parties were famous. Locals would attend as well as guests from hundreds of miles around, often arriving via boat, and the bay would swarm with yachts dotting the water.

These were the idle rich, business scions and timber barons, old money descended from pioneer families. Among their many influential friends, the Palmers always made sure to invite my parents. They loved my parents, and having a concert pianist amongst their guests only added to the fun, while my sophisticated mother could let her hair down and have a good time.

Often my father would get coaxed into playing the old piano in Far-A-Way's vaulted living room, and he'd treat the guests to abridged versions of classical pieces, traditional favorites, and jazz standards as the festivities warmed up with good cheer and generous cocktails. As a regular at Far-A-Way, I knew that the piano was not only out of tune but several of the keys didn't even work. Yet somehow my father made it sing.

* * *

One party at Far-A-Way became particularly significant. This was the Fourth of July, when I was fifteen years old.

My family had recently moved to Fayetteville, Arkansas where my father had been offered a post as Professor and Chairman of Music at the University of Arkansas. I missed my life in Washington terribly, especially in the beginning, so it was with deep gratitude that I accepted an offer from Mrs. Palmer to come back and spend the summer at Far-A-Way with Margie.

For an entire week before the Fourth of July, we helped get the house ready for the impending festivities, scrubbing bathrooms and assisting Mrs. Ramsdell—the family's cook, whom I loved—in the kitchen. Margie and I had been staying upstairs on a sleeping porch, but as guests began to arrive, we were booted out of the main house to one of the cabins on the property.

On the day of the Fourth, hundreds of pleasure craft crowded in the bay fronting Far-A-Way, and the dock filled several rows deep with visiting guests' yachts and seaplanes. The biggest boats dropped anchor in the middle of the bay, far too large to use the dock, and mini parties began to break out on the fantails. Skiffs and shore boats ran constantly back and forth, ferrying guests to and from their yachts. Festivities were expected to continue late into the night.

The house and manicured grounds overlooking the bay teemed with guests. Bars had been set up in strategic spots both inside and outside, so wherever a guest turned, they'd find booze and a bartender dispensing it.

True to tradition, Mrs. Palmer had created a feast with the help of Mrs. Ramsdell. The table groaned with salads, desserts, and fried chicken that's still the best I've ever tasted. Earlier that morning, a few of us kids had been recruited to man the crank for homemade ice cream, which now found its way out of the deep freeze and served to the guests.

I spent most of the day with the son of one of the families in attendance—a sweet, handsome boy of seventeen. We managed to steal a few beers and some firecrackers, then we occupied ourselves out on the water, swimming and boating with Margie and a few other friends.

As evening approached, the boy and I headed back to the house to find a good spot for the fireworks. Many of the guests returned to their boats to watch from their decks out on the bay. As soon as the sun had sunk below the tree line, a giant boom sent shockwaves across the harbor. Mr. Palmer had fired his solid brass cannon, announcing the commencement of the show.

Longbranch's local fire chief, who'd been invited for this very purpose, waddled to his station and, with the wave of his hand, directed his team of volunteer firefighters to begin. Patriotic music blared from speakers as one rocket after another shot into the air, bursting into glittering explosions of color and sound.

It was an ideal romantic moment. In fact, this party marked the first time my path crossed with that of the man I'd go on to marry—the man who would stand by my side as my life shattered apart due to unthinkable revelations within my family, the man who'd painstakingly help me piece it back together.

But he wasn't the nice boy with whom I viewed the fireworks. The man I'd marry was, at that moment, not even watching the show.

He was passed out in one of the cabins, drunk from the booze that had been handed out like water all day long.

\* \* \*

Don had recently met Clarke Palmer at a Marine Corps reserve meeting on the very day that Don swore in for service. Eighteen years old and with the draft on his heels, Don wanted to join the Marines—his top pick—while he still had a choice.

Clarke, who'd been released from his own active duty not long before, gave Don some advice. "Go to Canada," Clarke said.

Don laughed.

Don had a girlfriend named Libby he'd met while attending Seattle University, who was back in North Hollywood visiting her family. She also happened to be a friend of Clarke's—truly everyone was a friend of Clarke's—and Clarke had heard about Don from her. He invited Don to come up to Far-A-Way sometime, but Don politely declined. He didn't tell Clarke that the idea of being trapped for a weekend with a bunch of strangers sounded, to him, like torture.

A few weeks later, Don's mother informed him that Clarke had called the house to invite him to the Fourth of July party at Far-A-Way. Before Don could decline, she said that he'd actually made her promise he would go. A little annoyed, since Don was set to leave for active duty less than a week after the holiday and already had much weighing on his mind, but not wanting to be responsible for breaking his own mother's promise, Don reluctantly agreed. He convinced his friend, Mike, to join him, and after returning from a weekend on the Washington Coast, the two friends drove the forty-or-so miles from Tacoma to Longbranch on the day of the Fourth.

Pulling up to the house, Don and Mike were thunderstruck by their first sight of a Far-A-Way party. As Don took it in, still trying to believe his eyes, Clarke appeared to welcome them. He told Don he had someone he wanted Don to meet.

Clarke signaled to a figure nearby, and Don was thunderstruck all over again. It was Libby, his girlfriend. Clarke had paid to fly her up from North Hollywood just to surprise Don, a guy he barely knew.

That, in a nutshell, was Clarke.

Don couldn't believe it. Quickly he realized that's why his mother had been so adamant about Don attending. Clarke must have pulled her in on his scheme.

With Libby by his side, Don knew he couldn't let this celebration go to waste, and the two of them entered the grounds of Far-A-Way.

\* \* \*

While I ran around the property, swimming and sneaking a few fire-works, Don and Libby really lived it up. Some of the men had taken it on themselves to push booze on attendees. "Try this," they'd say while handing Don a drink, then they'd make a new cocktail before he could finish the first. "This one, too."

Both nineteen years old, neither Don nor Libby had had much experience with hard liquor, and it wasn't long before they felt the effects. Somewhere in all their merriment, they must have lost track of each other.

Margie and I found the poor girl passed out on the ground near the cabins. We'd seen her earlier in the company of Don—a guy we didn't know—so we sent one of Margie's siblings to find him.

When Don arrived, he seemed to be holding his liquor at least slightly better than her. He quickly scooped Libby up in his arms and carried her to the main house in search of a room for her to sleep it off.

I couldn't help but notice how strong and capable he looked as he carried her away. *That's a man,* I thought. *That's not a boy.*

\* \* \*

Later, with festivities nearing an end, Margie and I returned to our cabin to change out of our wet bathing suits. As we undressed, I caught a familiar whiff in the air. Alcohol.

I turned, trying to place the source, and that's when I noticed someone was asleep in my bed.

Instantly Margie and I screamed bloody murder and grabbed up our suits and towels, covering ourselves as we ran, still screaming, to the other room. "There's a man in my bed!" I shrieked.

At the sound of our screams, Don—who'd stumbled into what he thought was a vacant cabin looking for a place to sleep off the booze—was roused from the depths of unconsciousness. Even in his alcohol-addled mind, he thought he saw the half-clothed figures of two terrified girls sprinting out of the room.

In a panic, he shot out of bed and got out of there as fast as he could.

By the time Margie and I had the nerve to peek around the corner, we found the room completely deserted.

Outside, Don ran to find Mike and told him they had to leave—now! They jumped in their car and high-tailed it back to Tacoma, Don vowing he'd call Libby to explain the next morning once she was awake. He'd had way too much partying for one night.

❋ ❋ ❋

It wasn't until seven or eight years later, after Don and I had "met" through our now mutual friend Clarke and started dating, that we compared stories from Far-A-Way and figured out that I was the girl in the cabin, and Don was the guy in my bed. We could hardly believe the coincidence.

So manifests the fairy-tale magic of Far-A-Way.

❋ ❋ ❋

When Ted began dating a woman from a wealthy family in the San Francisco area, he wanted to bring her around, so we could meet her. We still had the cabin then—this was right before we moved—and Ted arranged for them to drive up for the day.

John and I had spent the morning out on the beach, so we were wearing grubby old clothes when Ted's car pulled in. I have a vivid memory of Ted and a stylish woman stepping out as John and I approached.

Ted seemed nervous. His girlfriend was beautiful with long, dark hair and an unmistakable air of sophistication. I didn't care that I was wearing grubby clothes. My experiences meeting people from all circles had left me comfortable in any company. We greeted them warmly and shook hands.

Ted couldn't wait to introduce his guest to my parents, which he did each in turn. Here was my mother, who came from a prominent Philadelphia family. There was my father, the renowned pianist.

Ted beamed. "I'd like you to meet my girlfriend," he said.

❋ ❋ ❋

As the day progressed, it grew obvious that Ted was hoping to impress her. He proudly took her around the property, showing her all his favorite spots, and told her about our travels in Europe.

We took them out on a boat, and Ted pointed out Far-A-Way, of which we had a perfect view from the water.

\* \* \*

Ted asked my father if he'd play something. The request was typical for my father, and he never minded it. He always had something he was busy working on, whether a new composition or a piano concerto for an upcoming performance, and he happily shared.

We followed my dad into his studio. Stepping in always felt like entering a different world—the world of my father. In the corner, a fire crackled inside a Franklin stove. One entire wall stood covered in shelves full of sheet music—just hundreds and hundreds of pieces. On another wall, a window looked out over Puget Sound through the trees.

And, of course, there was my father's grand piano. My father always taught us that musical instruments have histories. This particular Bechstein had been smuggled out of Nazi Germany—I have no idea how anyone could have managed this, but I was so grateful. I loved that piano. Years later when my dad eventually sold it and replaced it with a Bösendorfer, even though he went to great pains to put it in a good home where it would be appreciated, still I cried.

That day, we crowded around the piano like an altar. John and I made sure to let Ted and his guest stand in front where they could watch my father's hands.

Wearing old shorts and beach attire, my father sat at the Bechstein, put his hands on the keys, and he began. Music filled the air, and I marveled, as I always did, that my dad could do something like that.

While he played, I glanced over at Ted's face. He wasn't watching my father or his hands as they danced over the keys. Ted was watching his girlfriend.

*This is my family*, it seemed he wanted her to know. *This is why I deserve you.*

*Edna in Fayetteville, Arkansas.*

# No, It's Cute

In 1969, Ted visited us in Arkansas. By then my family had lived in Fayetteville for a little over three years—long enough for my fellow classmates at school to finally stop calling me "that new girl."

Arkansas was to be a stopover, Ted said when he made arrangements with my father, a brief sojourn on his way to Philadelphia. There, in the land of his birth, he'd stay with his Aunt Audrey (Louise's sister) and cousin Bruce for six months and attend classes at Temple University, all while trying to learn more—if anything—about the identity of his biological father.

I don't know what narratives Ted told others about his origin. In fact, I can't say for certain what he told himself. Only much later did I learn that a question existed, to some outside the family, as to whether Louise was his mother or sister, and I can only chalk this up to what was fabricated in Philadelphia, prior to their move to Tacoma, in order for Louise to avoid scandal as a single mother. I've come to learn that she briefly changed their last name to Nelson, seemingly to make it appear that she'd been married. I assume the question of her being Ted's sister also sprang from an intent to evade gossip.

All I can say for certain is that while growing up with Ted, the situation was always straightforward and simple to us in the family. Louise was a Cowell by birth, and she was Ted's mother.

The question of Ted's father, though, remained a mystery.

Despite my dad's closeness with Louise, she'd never divulged to him any further details of Ted's conception, so we were just as in the dark as Ted. Frankly, I don't know why Louise never told Ted the identity of his biological father. His travels to Philadelphia, in search of traces of the man, prove it clearly bothered Ted. I believe it even angered him. Louise had to know he felt this way. Yet she continued to brush aside his questions, choosing instead to leave them unanswered.

I've since come to understand that as mothers, with the intention of protecting our children, we can only do our best. And, as I know too well, sometimes our best intentions are flawed. When does shielding a child become withholding? It's a question I'd grapple with myself years later when, much like Louise, I'd be forced to face the issue of what to tell—or not tell—my own child of her knotty family tree.

* * *

When Ted arrived at the house, we greeted him like one of us—that's what he was, after all. As he stepped into the foyer, I remember the sensation of familiarity, which I found comforting. His easy smile and distinct gait provided a link to my beloved life and memories back in Washington.

My parents and I showed him all around our home, even pointing out my mother's bidet, a luxury she'd come to value from our time in Paris. In the living room we asked what Ted thought of the new furniture and custom drapes, upgrades paid for with the insurance money after a faulty floor lamp ignited the old curtains in the room. I told Ted the story, reenacting my horror when I walked in and saw flames engulfing the entire wall along with my father's beloved Bechstein grand piano—the latter of which we were able to put out with extinguishers and old army blankets.

Ted laughed at our dramatization of the story and admired the newly restored piano, testing out a couple keys. Though he must have been tired from hours of travel, he showed no interest in resting. His stay with us would be short—only a couple of days—and it felt to us that he didn't want to waste any of it.

We knew Arkansas was a significant detour for Ted. It meant hundreds of additional miles. But the inconvenience was worth it to him. With the house tour finished, we sat around the dining table, chatting and catching up, enjoying the comfortable happiness of being united again.

* * *

With John away at grad school and my parents busy with obligations, it fell to me to entertain Ted the following day. Grabbing the keys to my parents' Buick, I told him to come with me. "I'll show you around," I said.

As a senior in high school, the five years between us didn't feel so significant anymore, and Ted seemed amused as he followed me out to the car. "You drive now, huh?" he said.

Truth was, I loved driving. As a kid it had been boats and horses, but once I got my driver's license, there'd been no stopping me. To this day, I've never met a vehicle I couldn't—and didn't want to—drive.

As I steered the Buick onto the road and began telling Ted what I had planned for the day, I caught him staring at me, smiling.

"What?" I asked.

"Nothing," Ted said. "It's just that you've picked up a little bit of an accent. A Southern drawl."

Outraged, I told him that was impossible. I spoke the same way I'd always spoken; he just didn't remember correctly.

"No," Ted said, laughing, "it's cute."

* * *

Though Ted's appearance hadn't changed much—indeed I found comfort in his familiarity—I know the same couldn't be said of me. Teenage years do a lot to a girl, and I'd experienced my share of metamorphosis.

One such transformational event had occurred shortly after we moved. Though I'd come to love Fayetteville, leaving my beloved Puget Sound for steamy, bug-filled Arkansas had been tough. And I wasn't the only one in the family who found the transition challenging.

My mother had left behind her family and support system, and she struggled with the new southern climate. So, when she complained of a headache one afternoon while my father was in New Mexico for a work retreat, I figured it was the humidity.

But the next morning before I left for school, I could see my mom was very ill. She couldn't get out of bed, and while I talked with her, she kept briefly passing out, her pupils rolling backwards until all I saw were the whites of her eyes.

My father's work retreat had taken him onto a mountainside in Taos where I knew he didn't have access to a telephone. Without him to turn to, I had to handle this on my own. But I was only fourteen, and I'd never dealt with a health crisis before. I could feel a cold panic rise up inside me, but I tamped it down.

Frantically, I called my mother's doctor and described her symptoms. He didn't sound concerned and sent over a prescription for nausea. I explained that this seemed more serious than nausea, but he dismissed my worries. "The pharmacy will be there soon with the pills."

I tried to take comfort in his lack of concern, but still I stayed home from school to be there when the pills arrived and keep an eye on my mother.

The pills came, and they were useless. My mother continued to pass in and out of consciousness.

I called the doctor again. If I'd been keeping a lid on my panic before, now it came bursting out. I'm sure he could hear it in my voice, but he ignored my pleas. Instead, he ordered more pills—this time for dizziness—again to be delivered by the pharmacy.

When they arrived, I rushed them to my mother, but by then she was so far out of it, I couldn't even get her to take them.

The phone rang, and I rushed to answer it. It was the vice principal from my school calling about my absence. In a rush, I told him about my mother and begged him for advice. "Please," I said, "something's wrong with her." I desperately needed an adult to take charge and tell me what to do.

But instead, he merely scolded me for skipping school and ordered me to get to class immediately. I told him I couldn't leave my mother, so he asked to speak with her. At that moment, my mom was completely unconscious. "She can't talk," I said, reiterating that this was the problem.

Still, he refused to understand. He told me I was using my mother as an excuse to miss school, and there was an implied accusation—I sensed it even through my fug of panic—that my mother was drunk. When I hung up, I don't know if I was more relieved or panicked to end the call.

*No one believes me*, I remember thinking. I realized then that I couldn't rely on anyone else to take charge. I had to act, to take matters into my own hands. Gathering my courage, I ran to the neighbor's house and pounded on their door.

"I need an ambulance," I called out.

* * *

When the medics arrived, they couldn't get a gurney through the door and had to carry my mother out in a chair. I still remember how she looked as they hoisted her through the doorway. I couldn't take my eyes off her.

At the hospital, I paced the waiting room, alone and scared. *What if she dies?* I thought. *What if it's just me and my dad at home now?*

I could hardly comprehend this possibility for myself, let alone for my father. She was his high school sweetheart, his foundation. I knew he'd never be able to cope without her.

These thoughts were interrupted by the appearance of the ER doctor, and I rushed over to meet him. He told me that my mother had had a brain aneurysm, that pressure had been building in her brain, but they'd performed a spinal tap to reduce it. If I'd waited even ten more minutes to get her to the hospital, he said, my mother most likely would have died.

I simply didn't know how to process this information. The relief I felt was rivaled only by my fury of what could have been. The ER doctor patiently allowed me to vent my frustration of the day's events, creasing his forehead in genuine concern at my revelations, and I felt—finally— that I was being listened to. He treated me like a peer, and after bearing the weight of my decisions that day, I felt I'd earned it. Later when I saw the relief in my father's eyes, and even more so when I learned my mother's doctor—the one who'd sent the useless pills—lost his medical license due to a pattern of bad judgment calls, my feeling of responsibility deepened.

Before that experience, I'd been a child. In a matter of hours, I'd been forced to lose my naiveté and step up as an active member of the adult world.

* * *

Of course, other changes had occurred during Ted's and my time apart, some more outwardly obvious. I found the late 1960s to be a particularly exciting and transformative, if complicated, time to be a woman.

When I'd first started as a sophomore at Fayetteville High School, all the girls wore dresses or skirts with nylons. Competition to keep up with the styles had been fierce, our mascaraed eyes darting around the school hallways to spot who wore the latest trends and who fell behind. But by 1969 when Ted visited, dress standards for women had relaxed significantly. Almost overnight, we began wearing bell bottom jeans and T-shirts. Our rigid, patent-leather pumps were replaced by moccasins. And, with relief, we stopped caring so much about what the other girls wore.

I grew my hair long. I smoked weed with two of my girlfriends for the first time, potent stuff scored from a guy who'd brought it back from Vietnam; it left us so wasted it actually frightened us until we got the giggles at the local donut shop. I acquired, and dropped, a few boyfriends.

In short, I'd done quite a bit of growing up. So, without John or the other Bundy kids around, that day marked the first time that Ted and I ever hung out—really—as equals, as the updated iterations of ourselves, and we established a new era and a new closeness in our friendship.

Or, that's what I thought anyway, until I was forced to wonder if I ever really knew Ted at all.

\* \* \*

I turned on the radio and steered us toward the center of town.

Nestled amongst the Ozarks, Fayetteville is a pretty college town filled with tree-lined streets and stately brick buildings. Home of the University of Arkansas, the town is a relatively liberal enclave in the red state and a picture of culture and elegance. Reaching the downtown district, we passed the old post office and bank, the JCPenney and theater. "Seems like a nice place," Ted said.

I drove Ted past my high school and told him about my friends and how good the public education was in this college town where professors' families demanded high quality academics. I told him about the Language Club, of which I was president, and about my participation in the student pep club called the Peppers.

Ted talked about his time at Stanford the previous summer, where he'd earned a scholarship to study Chinese. He recounted stories about volunteering on the presidential campaign of Nelson Rockefeller, which gave him the opportunity to attend the 1968 Republican National

Convention in Miami. Though I skewed more politically left even as a teenager, that did nothing to deter my pride in Ted's many accomplishments and so obviously bright future.

Turning the Buick away from town, I took us on one of my favorite drives through the Ozarks, winding over roads through ethereal green forests that broke onto vistas of fields and valleys dotted with farmhouses skirted in porches. As we drove, the radio played Creedence Clearwater Revival and Joni Mitchell, "Mrs. Robinson" and "Sitting on the Dock of the Bay." That day Ted and I spent hours side-by-side in the car, and we never ran out of things to talk about.

Yet, when I look back now, what I find most interesting is all we didn't say.

\* \* \*

On a grand scale, we never brought up the topic of the Vietnam War. This seems, in hindsight, like a glaring omission. It's impossible to overstate the significance of the war to the American people in 1969. It fundamentally changed the culture around us. The subjects of the movies at the local theater we drove past that day, many of the songs broadcasting over the Buick's radio, even the bell bottoms and T-shirt I wore—all these could be traced to the influence of the war.

And it wasn't a distant adult problem. The Vietnam War was an issue for Ted's and my generation, and it hit close. Too damn close. I remember the first time I heard that guys I knew—guys I'd gone to high school with before they graduated—went overseas to fight.

I remember seeing one guy come back in a wheelchair.

I remember more who didn't come back at all.

Personally, I can attest it was a subject of great passion. In the years to come, I'd attend countless protests and help launch an underground newspaper at the University of Arkansas called *The Grapevine*, committed to publishing students' alternative views on the war and other issues.

In 1969 when Ted visited, the draft had already been in effect for several years, calling men of fighting age to mandatory military service unless they qualified for deferment. Though Ted had been granted a 2-S student deferment, he'd have been otherwise eligible and likely sent to boot camp. I have to imagine, especially with his interest in politics, he had a lot of thoughts and opinions on the topic himself.

But though we sang along to the radio that day—many songs likely referencing the war explicitly—we didn't discuss it.

Neither did we talk about the tensions in the South, the very region we drove through, still only five years after the passage of the Civil Rights Act. When I drove Ted past the University of Arkansas, I pointed out the buildings where my father taught and performed concerts. But I didn't mention the African American student groups who were fighting to change racist traditions, or how my father, as the Chairman of the Music Department, had sympathized with them and banned the playing of "Dixie" by the marching band. I didn't tell Ted about the blowback that had resulted from some in the community.

That day, I didn't confide to Ted that, though I knew I had more opportunities as a woman than my mother's generation, I'd come to understand they came with a dark price tag, an undercurrent of hostility. I'd felt it, especially in the tradition-loving South, on occasions such as the morning of my mother's aneurysm when men in authority refused to believe me, or even on another instance around the same time period, when I challenged a group of guys to a game of HORSE in an attempt to make friends. After I won, they took their ball and left me standing alone on the court. When school started a few weeks later, I learned they belonged to the varsity basketball team, and they made a point to ignore me for most of the year. It seemed they wanted me to know that by beating them, I'd stepped out of line.

For his part, Ted didn't confide in me that he'd very recently broken up with his longtime girlfriend, whom he'd hoped to marry. He didn't tell me that the ending of their relationship had left him shamed, shattered, maybe worse.

Neither did he tell me any details about his search for his biological father, nor what he hoped he'd find. He didn't discuss with me the absence he clearly felt.

And of course, Ted never got close to mentioning any inner demons, though by 1969 I have to think they'd presented, but to what degree I'll never know.

As I drove Ted around, showing off picturesque Fayetteville and the surrounding region, navigating past any shadows, I believe we set the model for our relationship. To Ted, I was "cute," a little sister-type figure, and our dynamic was always light and playful. I populated the idyllic side of Ted's personality, as sunny and glossy as a postcard.

Perhaps, like his mother who refused to talk about his birth father, Ted had learned to exhibit a reality devoid of impurities or complicated truths. From their brief name change to Nelson, Ted had been taught the value of presenting his best face, even if it was a lie.

That he had another side, I never would have suspected. I came to find out this was a talent of Ted's. He proved extraordinarily proficient at compartmentalization, keeping unseen elements of his character firmly guarded.

Of course, this skill would later enable him to lead his terrible double life.

＊ ＊ ＊

Before heading home, I drove Ted to the Vic-Mon, one of those old drive-in burger joints that now seem to exist only in summer towns and movies. In high school, the Vic-Mon was a favorite student hangout, the place to see and be seen. Always swarming with rich boys in the muscle cars bought by their daddies and beaters crammed full with teenagers— hunting in packs or on double dates—half the fun was driving around the place to find an empty spot and see who was present.

Once we pulled in, I rolled down the window and ordered from a speaker, waving to friends who spilled from their vehicles to circulate from car to car, flirting and shooting the breeze.

As Ted and I sat in the car eating french fries and drinking Dr. Peppers, I kept the window down so we could chat with neighbors from other cars who came by to say hello.

"This is Ted," I told them proudly, "my cousin from Seattle."

They stooped in through the open window to shake Ted's hand or maybe just to get a better look at the handsome stranger, shielding their eyes against the perfect sunny day. "Glad to have you in town," they said to Ted with the manners the region is known for. "You're mighty welcome."

*Edna's dad conducting a choir rehearsal in his home studio, Fayetteville, Arkansas*

*Edna and Jeanie at the Grand Canyon*

# Due Northwest

The car's hood popped open with a groan. I didn't bother to look down at the engine but kept my eyes trained on the lined, grease-caked face of the mechanic. *Please, don't frown*, I silently urged him. *We don't have time for whatever a frown means.* We had to meet my parents in San Francisco that evening, and we were still in Santa Maria, hours away. Even worse, since my parents were on the road themselves, we had no way to get in touch with them.

Jeanie and Margie stood beside me. We'd only just picked up Margie that morning from her Los Angeles suburb after days of driving from Arkansas, but already she looked as road-haggard as Jeanie and me.

By then, the Opel Kadett was five years old. John, who'd moved back to Seattle after finishing his master's degree, desperately needed a car, so my parents had formulated a grand idea. Since I was headed to Seattle myself to finish my schooling at the University of Washington, we might as well load up both their Buick and the Opel and drive two cars across the country with me. Then the Opel would stay in Washington with John.

If, of course, we could get it there.

*  *  *

This was the summer of 1972, and I'd just wrapped up my sophomore year at the University of Arkansas. My experience as a college student in Fayetteville had been rich, filled with political rallies, football mania, rock and roll, and a whirl-wind romance or two.

But in those last few weeks, I'd barely been able to focus on my studies, my mind drawn like the arrow on a compass to the Pacific Northwest where I'd soon be headed: back to the cool evenings and long northern days, back to my brother and my old friends, back to Longbranch.

This also meant I'd be able to reconnect with my cousin Ted, who lived not far from the UW campus where I'd be completing my junior and senior years.

Of course I'd miss Fayetteville and all the people there. I'd miss writing for *The Grapevine* and meeting the bands that my team of promoters helped bring to campus (BB King had even introduced me to his guitar, Lucille). I'd miss passing my dad on campus, smiling at his retinue of admiring students and his newly grown-out hair. But at the age of twenty, I longed to begin a new chapter in my life. I longed to return to Washington.

My parents had born the news about as well as I could hope. With carefully composed faces, they'd helped me pack up all my possessions into a few suitcases and prepare to leave Arkansas. My move represented a turning point in their lives as well as mine. Their last child was leaving the nest. Now, they'd be on their own.

I ground my teeth as I thought about them reaching San Francisco and waiting for us to meet them as arranged. I knew they'd be absolutely sick with worry.

I needed to get us back on the road as quickly as possible.

\* \* \*

Looking back, I guess I should be amazed the Opel got us as far as it did.

The car was a cute little thing that I'd used throughout high school, so I'd become intimately familiar with its under-powered engine and finicky stick shift. I've always had a real affinity for cars, so I'd grown accustomed to its quirks, and I was only happy to take on the job of driving it across the country.

But twenty-two hundred miles is agonizingly long, so I'd cast a net amongst friends to see if I could bring on another driver to help spell me. Thankfully, my good friend Jeanie had volunteered, lured by the promise of adventure.

There was only one problem. Jeanie didn't have much experience driving a stick.

It had been trial by fire as she gamely threw herself into the task. And the farther west we got, the better she became.

Across interstates and down main streets, over plains and mountains, we followed behind my parents in their blue Buick Special. Jeanie would do freeways, the long stretches in fourth gear, and I'd take over when we went through cities and towns when more shifting was required.

We were pounded by storms in Oklahoma, so fierce at times that visibility became impossible, hailstones so big I worried they'd break the windshield. In Albuquerque we stopped at Old Town to walk around art galleries and marvel at the dryness of the air. At the Grand Canyon, my parents decided we were too close not to see Las Vegas. It was a summer day in the Nevada sun with temperatures reaching 104 degrees. Their Buick had air conditioning; the Opel did not. By the time we reached the glittery city in the desert, Jeanie and I were fried.

After that, it was down to Southern California, where we'd arranged to pick up my childhood friend Margie, who'd be joining us for the drive to San Francisco before catching a bus back home. After a visit with Margie's mom in Canoga Park, we parted ways with my parents. They preferred to take a more direct route to San Francisco while we three girlfriends wanted to drive up the infamous Highway 1—a scenic road hugging the coastline that offered stunning views of the Pacific Ocean.

Of course, it was only after waving goodbye to my parents and commencing our trip unchaperoned when the Opel's engine began to give out. Somewhere around Santa Maria, I pulled over to the first auto repair shop I saw.

\* \* \*

The mechanic leered at us from over the hood. For the first time, it struck me how vulnerable we were, three women in our early twenties, miles from anywhere, with a busted car. I tried to swallow the thought. Because the Opel was my family's car, I felt responsible for the group. I needed to exude capability and strength. I needed to get us to San Francisco.

Over the hood, the man held up his grease-stained hands for us to see. "Would any of you girls sleep with a man who had hands like these?"

I have no idea what kind of response he was expecting, but the one he got was three women simultaneously recoiling backwards. The time had come for me to step up as the self-imposed leader, and with a voice that I hoped sounded both polite and forceful, I uttered, "No, thank you!"

Without batting an eye, he carried on with his assessment of the engine. And that's when I saw it, exactly what I'd dreaded.

He frowned.

The mechanic looked back up at us like a doctor with a terminal patient. There were major problems that needed addressing, he said. But considering our circumstances, he could make a few tweaks that would buy us some miles.

I anxiously approved, and the mechanic did his thing, then he sent us on our way.

Engine humming, I climbed in behind the wheel, and he closed the door behind me. He leaned down to the open window, and I could feel the three of us brace ourselves for his parting words.

"Whatever you do" he said, "just don't shut it off."

* * *

As soon as we pulled away from the shop, we all burst out laughing.

"What a creep," Margie said.

"At least he got the car running," I said as I navigated us back on the highway. By then it was midday, and we were way behind schedule.

I pressed my foot harder on the gas, and my blood went cold as I felt the engine resist. It might have been running, but the Opel was clearly still having trouble. I had to be very careful on how and when I shifted, and no matter what, it refused to go above forty miles per hour.

It was a tense drive. The already fussy engine had become even more demanding, so I needed to be the one behind the wheel for the duration. With white knuckles, I pushed as fast as the engine could muster, up the winding roads on what was meant to have been a relaxing drive.

Hours later as the sun set, the scenery we'd been looking forward to was masked in darkness.

A big part of what makes Highway 1 so breathtaking is its dramatic placement along the mountainside, the narrow road hugging a wall of rock on the right and a long drop to the Pacific Ocean on the left. Absolutely stunning in the daylight.

Treacherous in the dark.

So with tempers and engine straining, we limped through Big Sur in the pitch darkness, navigating hair-raising twists and turns, never knowing if the Opel would suddenly decide to throw in the towel.

The hour grew later and later. I cracked a window to feel the cool air on my face. I had to keep from getting sleepy. I had to stay alert.

By the time we staggered into San Francisco, it must have been after 1:00 a.m., and we were completely drained. My parents had been practically pulling out their hair with worry, and my dad met us in the hotel's parking lot in slippers and a bathrobe over his pajamas. We stopped the Opel in a parking space, and when we tried to move it again, the engine wouldn't start.

The mechanic was right. It was done.

We had to have it towed the next day.

\* \* \*

Margie had already purchased her bus ticket back to Los Angeles, so after very little sleep, we took her to the bus station the following day.

"So much for a relaxing road trip," I said as I hugged her goodbye.

Margie laughed and brushed it off, reminding me how much fun we'd have in a couple short months. She'd be joining me in Seattle in September, where I'd enrolled for the fall quarter at the University of Washington while Margie planned to settle in and work before starting classes herself the following year.

I eagerly agreed, and we all waved goodbye as she climbed the stairs of the bus and rode away, back down the coast.

After three days of sightseeing in San Francisco while the Opel's engine got a complete overhaul (I can only hope my parents' relief at our safety took some sting off the bill) our small caravan continued the journey north.

Finally, we arrived in Seattle.

Seeing the city again, I was overcome with a sense of coming home. There was nowhere else in the world I wanted to be, and I couldn't wait for the next phase of my life to begin.

This was the summer of 1972. Over the next three years, the entire region would become engulfed with fear, the hunting ground of a serial killer. And I'd have a front row seat.

*Edna and Don*

# Saturday in the Park

My parents could only stay in Seattle for a day or two before my father's duties obliged them to gas up their Buick again and embark on the long drive back home. But since Jeanie didn't need to be back at the University of Arkansas until mid-August, she planned to stay with me in Seattle for a few more weeks. As I didn't yet have a place to live, the two of us crashed on the couch of Don's old friend, Mike.

Mike rented a house near Green Lake, just north of the University District (referred to as the U-District by locals). That summer, his place became quite the gathering spot. Friends dropped by in what seemed like a continuous parade, and Jeanie and I were delighted to be right in the middle of the action.

Since it was Don who'd arranged our stay with Mike, it came as no surprise when, not long after we'd settled in, he showed up at the house along with Clarke.

I'd connected with Don two summers earlier during a trip back to Longbranch. By then, he was in the Marine Corp Reserves and had become one of Clarke's best friends. In anticipation of my visit, Clarke hyped both of us up to one another (of course, we didn't know then that our paths had already crossed that fateful July Fourth when I was fifteen). The hype worked. The moment I laid eyes on Don, I fell hard. He told me later that he did, too. We spent the rest of my visit seeing each other as much as possible, and even after I had to leave, Don made a trip all the way to Arkansas to see me. Our connection was electric. The air practically sizzled when we were together.

But still, two years had passed, and we'd been separated by thousands of miles, in touch only sporadically through letters penned by

*Don (right) with best friend Clarke Palmer (left).*

Mike, Don's appointed Cyrano since he didn't feel he was any good at writing. We'd never given our relationship a label, and both of us had dated other people.

I found out later that Don was nervous to see me again. I felt it, too, but I was also fresh out of a recent relationship in Fayetteville and wary of diving into big emotions again for a while.

We made arrangements to tag along with Clarke to spend the next afternoon at a party on his friend's houseboat on Lake Union. Seattle has an incredible houseboat community, made famous by the movie *Sleepless in Seattle*. And this houseboat where we'd be partying was particularly special, having been designed by a childhood friend from my Longbranch days, renowned architect and Seattle native, Jim (Jimmy) Olsen. I looked forward to the day. Don looked forward to the day.

It didn't go as either of us expected.

Don remembers it better than I do. According to him, everyone was drinking beer and having a good time, so—filled with good humor and liquid confidence—he came onto me too strongly. I remember feeling put off by his approach, thinking it was too much too soon.

Don says I rejected him. I don't remember that, exactly. But I do remember that he made me laugh. I liked that. Something must have given him a glimmer of hope, because before Jeanie and I left, Don asked if he could stop by Mike's the next day, and I agreed.

After we took off, Clarke and Don made the drive back to Tacoma, and Clarke spent the entire ride consoling Don that he hadn't totally blown it. Despite Clarke's best reassurances, Don wasn't convinced. He vowed to take it easy with me from then on.

❊ ❊ ❊

The next morning when he came by, Don scolded himself as he walked to Mike's front door. He needed to keep himself in check. He needed to play it cool and keep some distance.

But as soon as I answered the door, it was obvious I was very happy to see him, and Don's resolve crumbled. It was a perfect summer day, and he asked if he could take me out for a drive. I took one look at his cool '65 sky-blue Pontiac Bonneville convertible parked outside and eagerly accepted.

What can I say? I've always had a weak spot for cars.

That day we cruised all over the city with the Bonneville's top down. From Green Lake to Alki Beach, we soaked in the salty air and Seattle sun, laughing and enjoying the views.

And we talked. A lot. I remember opening up to Don on that drive, and him to me. By the time he dropped me back at Mike's, it was clear to both of us that we'd be seeing a lot more of each other.

And we did.

Being with Don felt familiar and right—and so much fun. Our relationship rekindled and quickly returned to the passion we felt when we first began dating two years earlier. We were together again because that's where we were meant to be.

I knew he truly loved me the day he allowed me and a couple girlfriends to put his hair up in rollers. He hated every second of it, but he did it because it made me laugh.

When we took out the rollers, Don had the perfect page boy hair style. He took one look in the mirror and recoiled in horror. We laughed our asses off while he ran to the shower to erase all trace of the crime.

I was smitten.

\* \* \*

On the Fourth of July, Ivar Haglund—owner of Ivar's Fish House—put on one of his monumental fireworks displays at Green Lake that he'd come to be known for. Don and I watched huddled together as swarms of fireworks shot into the sky and exploded, showering the horizon with fairy dust.

Our theme song became "Saturday in the Park" by Chicago, and to this day, whenever I hear it, I remember that summer. I was falling in love with my soulmate. It was a happy time.

I had no idea what was just around the corner.

\* \* \*

Being back in Seattle, I was eager to reconnect with my cousin Ted. At the time, he rented a room in a boarding house in the U-District, but he spent most of his time with his girlfriend, Liz.

Ted must have been eager to reconnect with me, too. Quickly after I arrived, Ted stopped by Mike's house with my brother, John.

Jeanie remembers the day well. The four of us went to Volunteer Park on Capitol Hill, and we walked around, playing word games and making each other laugh.

Ted appeared to be doing very well for himself at that time, and I don't think I'd ever seen him more driven. That summer, he'd been interning at Harborview Medical Center as a psychiatric counselor, but he talked more and more about getting involved again in politics.

Not long after that, Ted and Liz invited us to her house for dinner. Since we didn't have a car, Ted offered to come pick us up. Jeanie and I could see him pull up from the window as Ted parked his tan Volkswagen Beetle.

Piling into the car, I remember feeling awed at how grown up he seemed then, a proper adult hosting dinner parties. Liz had a young daughter, and together the three of them seemed to make a perfect family.

As we were invited into the house by Liz, Jeanie and I looked around in awe. A piano in the living room! A rug on the floor! To our young eyes, these indicated the peak of maturity. When Liz and Ted served us fresh peas and chicken for dinner, we couldn't have been more impressed.

Ted, it seemed, really had his life together.

❊ ❊ ❊

There are suspicions that Ted's documented murders—those that would start occurring soon—showed signs of prior training. Even the lead investigator on the case in King County, Detective Robert Keppel, would later go on record to say he believed Ted's methods in 1974 seemed too practiced to have been his first.

Much later, in the days leading up to his execution, Ted himself said he'd killed unidentified hitchhikers in the early 1970s, but much of his story, including dates, never fully added up, and I'm now loath to take anything Ted said strictly at face value.

So instead, I'm left to wonder. While I was busy falling in love and reestablishing myself in my beloved city, what was Ted doing in between our visits, when he made certain no one was watching?

❊ ❊ ❊

After several weeks in Seattle, Jeanie finally had to return home to Fayetteville for school, and I had to face the reality that I couldn't stay on Mike's couch forever.

Luckily, I managed to find a cute little rental on the top floor of a house in Wallingford, a short bus ride from campus. Originally a single residence, the attic had been converted into an apartment, and though the building was charming, sound proofing between the dwellings was non-existent.

I remember the first time I met my new downstairs neighbor, a woman named Mrs. Wortman. She had severely pulled-back hair, pursed lips, and an inquisitive thirteen-year-old son. She didn't bother to introduce herself or welcome me to the building. Instead, she just pursed those lips while, next to her, her son wouldn't stop staring.

With only a short time before classes were due to start, I bought a waterbed and a few pieces of furniture and set about trying to make the space my own.

But Mrs. Wortman downstairs, though out of sight, was my constant companion. Every sound in that building carried, and she had her ears carefully attuned. I couldn't even use the oven to make dinner without getting a *thump-thump-thump* from down below, her broom pounding the ceiling.

63

Margie often came by and stayed with me at the apartment. Don was also a regular visitor, and it wasn't unusual for him to bring along friends from high school and college roommates who'd become fellow Marines. *Pound-pound-pound.* The sound of Mrs. Wortman's broom handle became a chorus in the soundtrack to those days.

Looking back now, I can empathize with her. The woman must have lived her life in dread of me coming home, worse if I was accompanied by friends. As I went up and down that outside staircase, I'd routinely glance at her window, and more often than not I'd catch her beady eyes staring back through the curtain.

Her son was usually at a separate window pane, eyes wide, mouth agape. My social life had become his favorite form of entertainment, and his mother did not approve.

It finally came to a head one weekend. On Friday night, I went out with Don and some friends to the U-District, where I missed a step and managed to twist my ankle. As I tried to get up, it was clear I couldn't put any weight on it.

Don had to support me out to the car and drive me home, where he gently carried me up the staircase to my apartment. Sure enough, as we passed by the downstairs window, I glanced over in time to see the curtain move.

The next day, my ankle had swollen to twice its size and was starting to turn a troubling purplish-red. There was no way I could get up and down the stairs to my apartment. I, like the color of my ankle, was marooned.

One thing about Don, he's a problem solver. It didn't take him long to come up with the perfect solution. He called up his Marine Corps buddies and made a plan. They'd all take turns carrying me up and down the apartment's stairs, as needed. Along with Don, Clarke, Vic, and Doug signed up for duty to be my very own private elevator service. Problem solved.

After my third or fourth trip on the stairs, carried each time by a different, strapping young man in uniform, Mrs. Wortman had had enough. She was convinced I was turning tricks.

I got a call immediately from the landlord. He explained that he'd received angry complaints from the tenant downstairs, who was very concerned about my morals and the bad influence I was having on her son.

Even after I explained about my injury and why I needed help on the stairs, the landlord was not sympathetic. I wasn't a good fit, he said. I needed to leave. He admitted that there wasn't adequate soundproofing between the two units. "The next tenant will be someone without, ahem, a social life!"

Round one for Mrs. Wortman. I suspect she joined a prayer circle that night to give thanks.

* * *

So just like that, I was evicted. Homeless. Once Don got over his outrage at the landlord, he thought it was hysterical that I'd been kicked out for reasons that hinted I was a woman of loose morals, or—to use the word Mrs. Wortman would have preferred—a floozy. After all those nights of broom pounding and prying eyes at the window, I was actually relieved to get away.

But now classes would be starting in less than a month, and I had a bum ankle and no place to live.

Thankfully Margie and I joined forces. Together we found a great place even closer to campus in a brick building called Carter Hall Apartments. It only had one bedroom, which was allotted to me since I had a boyfriend, and Margie was a good sport to take the Murphy bed in the living room. But now we were right in the U-District, a short walk to our classes, close to grocery stores, restaurants, and anything else our young hearts desired.

Even better, the apartment was only a short walk away from Ted's boarding house. It wasn't long before he began stopping over to visit.

When I'd open the door to find Ted, he'd occasionally have a bag of groceries in his arms. "Let's make dinner," he'd say. I can't think of more welcome words to a poor, hungry college student.

If Margie was around, she'd be invited to join us, and we'd put something on the record player. Steely Dan, Stevie Wonder, or Chicago. Joni Mitchell or Cat Stevens. Sometimes, especially when I was missing my dad, I'd put on an LP of Vivaldi's *Four Seasons* or plug in a cassette he'd mailed to me of him playing the piano. Free from the listening ears of Mrs. Wortman, silence was rare in our apartment and avoided at all costs.

Ted was a thoughtful, if not inspired, cook. If he brought ingredients to make spaghetti, he'd make sure to include good bread and a bottle of wine, maybe even some cheese and fruit. We'd stand in the tiny kitchen, chopping and stirring, bumping into each other and talking about our days.

Ted had begun working for Governor Dan Evans's Washington State re-election campaign, where he'd already become a familiar face in the political scene, establishing a first-name-basis with bigwigs in local government as well as respected political reporters, such as Richard Larsen from the *Seattle Times*. Ted saw a future in politics, and he talked excitedly about the possibility of going to law school.

He said he wanted to make a difference. That year, he held positions in both Crime Prevention for the city and Justice Planning for the county, and he spoke about important work he hoped to accomplish with a study into violent assaults against women.

Looking back, these details leave me particularly disturbed. Even now, I'd like to believe Ted's heart was somewhere in the right place, that indeed his interest in preventing crimes, especially those against women, proved he actively sought to combat the demons he likely already knew lived inside of him.

Unfortunately, I'm inclined to believe that his good deeds were more deviously planned, that his true aim was to become better acquainted with law enforcement in order to pinpoint weaknesses that he could use to his advantage. I can imagine that his study into cases of violence against women only succeeded in arousing ideas.

But at the time, during those home cooked meals while he spoke passionately of his future plans, I felt admiration for my cousin whom I considered a champion for females. I remember thinking to myself, if Ted wasn't already in a committed relationship, I'd have tried to match him up with my friends.

* * *

After dinner, Ted would stay to help clean up, and we'd all dance around to the music.

I remember one night in particular, seared forever in my mind. Margie was home, and we were all kind of dancing to whatever was on the record player. I went to the window where we kept our records, and I thumbed through the stack for what to put on next. The current song was slower in tempo, and when I turned back to the room, I found Ted and Margie slow dancing.

Margie had her head leaned against Ted's chest, and as they turned with the music, I got a direct view of Ted. I could see him looking down at her.

I will never forget the look on his face.

Ted's jaw was clenched tight, and his usually blue eyes appeared coal black. I don't know how that was possible, yet that's what I saw. It was as if he was someplace else—a completely separate universe. For a moment, I swear, I didn't recognize him at all. It wasn't Ted. His countenance was tense. Mean.

"Ted," I said to get his attention, but he didn't hear me. "Hey, Ted?"

Finally he snapped out of it, and that terrible look evaporated into the air.

"Are you okay?" I asked, sincerely concerned.

Margie, who didn't see the way he'd been staring at her, stirred and looked up with interest.

But Ted just smiled, the old him again. "I'm fine," he said, still smiling, and he was so much himself again that I couldn't help but believe him. Everything was fine. Everything was normal.

Yet, I never forgot the incident.

Shortly after that, Ted said he needed to go and quickly left. I remember feeling surprised at his sudden departure.

I have no idea what might have occurred that night after he left my apartment. What he might have done.

# Letter from Edna to Ted in Prison

*Written after his execution date was set for July 2nd, 1986.*

*Transcription of entire letter.*

May 31st, 1986

Dear Ted,

All these years I have written you 100's of letters in my mind...only to tear them up in shreds of frustration. My emotions just didn't conform to the written word. I am not even sure if I will be successful this time. However, I feel that now is the time to say to you what I have been wanting to say to you over the course of these last 10+ years since I last saw you.

Ted, it took me a long time to accept the fact that someone I considered not only a close friend but occasionally a confidant capable of ever committing the acts of violence you are guilty of. Like everyone else near you, I saw only one side of you. The side I saw was loving, affectionate, intelligent, curious, ambitious...the positive aspects of your personality would go on and on.

So what happened? What happened to you, Ted, that you would develop such a deep rage...a deep hatred that you would feel overwhelmed to such an extent that you killed ruthlessly, in cold blood without mercy? I HATE YOU FOR WHAT YOU DID to those women/children and their families. So many times have I wanted to take hold of you and shake you... shake you until you'd break down and cry.

Were you taking revenge on your mother? On the rest of your family? On your biological father? On those girls who'd rejected you? Come on Ted... this is a cry from someone who still remembers the other Ted. Can you stop the pretense? It appears the end is near for you. I must confess to you that I will miss you...my great memories of you. But can you come to terms with what you have done? For the sake of your family and especially the families of your victims will you please explain what happened. Some of the women you murdered have never been found! Ted, you would be benefiting mankind by letting them understand better how a mind like yours works. It is time for you to do this. If you want to tell me, I'll be willing to come there...but only if you promise me...no games... no bullshit. You cannot deny your guilt...I am not interested in hearing excuses but would certainly be impressed if you could open those flood-gates that have been so tightly shut these past years.

What do you say, Ted? It's a chance for salvation. I'm sure of it. Ted, I'll never forget you...for the good memories. Unfortunately, I'll never forget the "other" you too.

Your Cousin,

Edna

*May 31st 1986*

*Dear Ted,*

*All these years I have written you 100's of letters in my mind...only to tear them up in shreds of frustration. My emotions just didn't conform to the written word. I am not even sure if I will be successful this time. However, I feel that now is the time to say to you what I have been wanting to say to you over the course of these last 10+ years... ever since I last saw you.*

*Ted, it took me a long time to accept the fact that someone I considered not only a close friend but occassionally a confidant capable of ever committing the acts of violence you are guilty of. Like everyone else near you, I saw only one side of you. The side I saw was loving, affectionate, intelligent, curious, ambitious... the positive aspects to your personality would go on and on. So what happened? What happened to you, Ted, that you would develop such a deep rage, a deep hatred that you would feel overwhelmed to such an extent that you killed ruthlessly, in cold blood without mercy? I HATE YOU FOR WHAT YOU DID TO those women/children and their families. So many times have I wanted to take hold of you and shake you...I'll shake you until you'd break down and cry. Were you taking revenge on your mother?... or*

*Edna and Don*

# Close to Home

The University of Washington was—and still is—a beautiful campus, perfectly situated to flaunt views of the Cascade Mountains across Portage Bay and Lake Washington. Mount Rainier looms in the distance, keeping watch over the school grounds like a lighthouse, and on clear days it appears so close you could reach out and touch it.

As classes began, I felt overwhelmed by UW's size, both in student body (at 40,000 students, it was four times larger than the University of Arkansas) and in geographic footprint. In one of his first orders of brotherly business, John helped me purchase a ten-speed bicycle, so I could get around the vast campus.

One morning I set off to check out a class that seemed potentially intriguing. I'd heard buzz about the professor, and the class would help me fulfill a requirement towards my BA degree. Nervous that I'd get lost, I gave myself ample time to get there, and I ended up arriving at the classroom far too early. I'm so glad I did.

Soon after I sat down, every other seat got snatched up, and then, as students continued to arrive, a standing line began to form along the back of the room. Unsure if I was even in the right classroom, I rechecked the class description. Sure enough, it was Irish History with Dr. Giovanni Costigan. Was it possible that this many people could be interested in Irish history?

The door opened, and a tiny, white-haired gentleman scurried inside. He wore a bow tie, and his arms were full of papers. Instantly the room went silent. *Who is this guy?* I wondered.

After arranging his papers on his desk, Dr. Costigan turned and addressed the class. The moment he spoke, he had us. He addressed us with such respect, it was impossible not to return it. But what really set him apart most was the way he taught.

Historical figures became real. Distant time periods became present. History, in his hands, was far more than a list of dates. He made it urgent, important, compelling. He made it come alive.

I found out that the previous year, Dr. Giovanni Costigan had debated William F. Buckley on the UW campus, a two-and-a-half-hour televised event that drew a larger audience than the Seattle SuperSonics game that same night. This man had a gift. I suppose it was no wonder his classes were so popular.

Over the next two years, I eagerly took all of Dr. Costigan's classes as well as several American History courses taught by another compelling professor, Jon Bridgeman. Almost before I knew it, I'd wracked up enough credits to graduate with a major in History. The subject became a passion that would carry through my entire life.

During this same time period, Ted began to use my beloved college campus and others in the surrounding area as his personal stalking ground, leading up to the murderous spree that would soon dominate the newsstands.

But as I sat in classes, listening to great scholars make history come alive, I couldn't have known that I was actually living in a moment soon to be included in the history books, and that I'd spend most of my life trying to stay out of them.

* * *

"Hey, where else do Seattle University students like to hang out?" Ted asked.

Ted and John had met up with Don for lunch at the Eastlake Zoo, a student-favorite tavern south of the U-District near Lake Union. Don told me about their boys' afternoon later, which seemed unremarkable at the time but has since become a memory that troubles him. Don said they'd just finished eating when Ted looked around at the mostly empty tables and posed Don the question about student hangouts.

Don signaled for the bill. "Well," he said. "I'll show you."

Don was a former student at Seattle U, just south of the University of Washington on the other side of Capitol Hill, so this happened to be a subject he knew well. Leaving the Zoo, he took Ted and John to the

Cellar Tavern, which, true to its name, was located downstairs from a street-level business off Madison Street very close to Seattle U's campus.

But still mid-afternoon, the Cellar didn't have much more action going on than the Zoo, and after poking their heads inside, the group quickly turned and left.

Undeterred, Don took them a couple blocks away to a bigger student bar called the Forum. Walking in, Don noted with satisfaction that the place was already packed with students.

The three of them found a table and ordered beers. Don tried to start up a game of pinball, but he couldn't keep Ted interested, even with the promise of winning tickets that could be cashed in for quarters at the bar.

Ted, Don said, didn't care about the pinball game or the tickets. He just wanted to people-watch.

After their second round of beers, they took off.

At the time, Don thought it was a nice day out with John and Ted, an opportunity to enrich his relationships with my family. Now when he thinks back, he says it gives him the creeps. He can't help wondering at Ted's true motivation to find bars that were popular with students.

Whatever Ted was playing at, Don feels disgusted at the idea that Ted dragged him into it.

\* \* \*

During my junior year, I thought it might be fun to sign up for a German class. Because of my time spent in Paris, I'd always taken French lessons, and I wanted to try something completely different. It was in that class where I met Tom, and we became fast friends. Tom was a member of the Husky Skydiving Club, having personally made over three-hundred free-fall jumps, and he badgered me to join up.

At first, I answered him with something like, "Why the hell would I do that?" So I was as surprised as anyone when, as the class began nearing its end, and Tom urged me again to join the Husky Skydiving Club, I looked at him and answered, "Why the hell not?"

For some reason, conscious or unconscious, it completely slipped my mind to inform my parents of my plans.

Before we were even allowed to look at a plane, about a hundred other skydiving hopefuls and I were put through two full weeks of ground school. There we learned how to fall (a PLF, or Parachute Landing Fall) and all about parachute safety.

The parachutes were not the more sophisticated ones used today. These were World War II–style, bulky, cumbersome things that were perfectly round in shape. If everything went according to plan, the chutes would release when triggered by a static line after we jumped. But if that didn't happen, we had to know how to manually engage the secondary chute. In those days, we jumped solo, even our first time, so there'd be no instructor strapped to me, helping as I plummeted through the air.

After two weeks of climbing towers and tumbling off, our jump was scheduled for the following afternoon. As I set about trying to remind myself why I'd agreed to do this, I was taken aside from the rest of the class. Our jumpmaster informed me that he'd been watching us all carefully in training. I seemed to understand the drills, I could execute them well, and—most importantly—I looked calm while doing so.

That was news to me. It must have been incredible acting on my part because I felt anything but calm.

The jumpmaster continued. They needed to designate someone to be the first jumper from the plane, someone who could get the ball rolling and who wouldn't back out at the last minute. Because if they didn't jump, no one else would be able to jump, and the whole plane would have to come back down.

He looked at me, and I knew the question was coming but still felt entirely unprepared for it. "Would you be the one to jump first?"

Immediately my stomach tied into knots. But I was also—God help me—flattered. I didn't know if I could do it, but he thought I could. I could rise to that.

So, with both total uncertainty but also something masquerading as certainty, I summoned whatever acting skills had gotten me into this mess and said yes.

❊ ❊ ❊

The next day we loaded into the plane late in the afternoon, the last sky diving group of the day. Tom had told me he'd be coaching me via walkie talkie from the landing zone, and I took some comfort in that.

Since I was jumping first, I had to wait to board last. I watched as my fellow jumpers awkwardly piled on their gear and loaded into the airplane, a single-engine Cessna commonly used for skydiving, and reality hit me. *What had I gotten myself into?*

Finally, it was my turn to load. Like my fellow jumpers, I awkwardly waddled aboard in my gear and hooked the static line of my main chute to the zipline on the plane's ceiling. It was this setup that would automatically tug open the chute once I jumped.

If I jumped.

I had to jump. I'd promised.

In the plane, the engine was deafeningly loud which made it impossible to communicate verbally, so we had to watch for signals. As I waited by the door, my heart pounded into my throat. The signal could come at any second. I watched.

It came. It was time.

Lugging my equipment, I stepped out onto the strut of the plane. I was actually *outside* the airplane! Wind whipped at me, flapping my cheeks and causing tears to streak from my eyes into my hair. I looked down at the ground below. This was it.

By that point, standing outside the aircraft, heart pattering a million miles a minute, I was ready—if only to put myself out of my misery. The jumpmaster hit my leg, prompting me to go.

I jumped.

Nothing could have prepared me for the sensation of falling at such a speed.

Almost right away, the static line engaged, and my chute opened. *Thank God it opened.* Just as fast as I'd been falling, suddenly I was yanked up by the parachute. I felt like a rubber band. But quickly equilibrium set in, and after the skull-rattling clamor of the plane engine, the world was suddenly, miraculously quiet.

Below, the earth stretched out, limitless. I could see everything. Up ahead, the San Juan Islands dotted the water. Farther I could see straight on to Canada. Dusk was turning the sky into a canvas of colors, and everything glowed.

It was so peaceful. Church-like. I remember passing by a bird flying through the air and feeling awed that we were sharing the same air space. *Maybe I'll come back as a bird*, I thought.

As if from a tunnel, I started to grow aware of a voice speaking to me. "Jumper number one," it crackled from the walkie talkie strapped to my chest. Tom had been trying to get my attention, but I was so overtaken by the experience, I hadn't noticed. Springing to action, I answered.

Through the radio, Tom gave me instructions on how to pull the risers, and he guided me right into the designated landing zone. As the ground rushed toward me, I knew I was coming in too fast to stay on my feet. With a final hard pull on both risers at once, the chute slowed me down just enough to execute a safe PLF, just like I'd practiced in training.

Rising up from the ground, I felt a rush of exhilaration. I'd faced terror unlike anything I'd known up to that point, and I'd survived, completely unhurt—and even in the designated landing zone! I wanted to go up and do it again!

Unfortunately, since it was so late in the day, that was impossible. I consoled myself that it was probably for the best. The forty-dollar price tag was a strain on my student budget. But still, the jump had taught me a lot about myself. If I could skydive, I could do just about anything.

I even called my parents to tell them about my jump. They bore the news with simultaneous shock and lack of surprise, since they knew me so well. Most of all, they were relieved I was okay. I told them I was more than okay.

I felt invincible.

* * *

After I raved to him about my jump, Don signed up to skydive with a small outfit out of Thun Field, south of Tacoma. His experience couldn't have been more different than mine.

They gave him no ground school. They gave him only minimal training.

In fact, they put him on a plane the same day he signed up, with a parachute too small for his size. Of the three people he jumped with, two of them ended up in the hospital with serious injuries, and Don should have gone as well. He landed hard and injured his back, an injury that still gives him problems to this day.

I sensed the groundwork forming for a belief that I'd bolster over the years. I didn't second-guess my own jump, but I grew more and more convinced of the importance of my training. Preparation was protection. The world was full of possibilities, but we had to be smart. I felt certain that was the lesson.

But then, there was also this:

Just a few weeks after I jumped, I learned my own jumpmaster and a plane full of parachutists were overtaken by fog, lost their bearings, and crashed into the side of a mountain. Everyone on board died.

That really shook me. Knowing what I did of them, I felt certain they'd been as prepared as possible. I knew they weren't foolish.

Some things you can never see coming.

My feeling of invincibility vanished.

* * *

During these years, Ted continued to drop by my Carter Hall apartment, and he was always a welcome guest. Even if we already had other people over, we never thought twice about inviting him inside. In fact, I think he even enjoyed having a crowd.

Five years older, he seemed to us so put-together with his stick-straight posture and a sweater often draped over his shoulders, indicators of the "grown up" world from whence he came. Working on the Dan Evans's campaign, Ted had quickly become a rising star in local politics, and we often urged him to regale us with behind-the-scenes tales of conventions and political events.

I remember one night he came over, and we got Ted talking about his most recent exploits on the campaign trail. He'd been doing "under-cover" work by attending rallies for Evans's opponent—sometimes wearing a wig and peppering the opposing candidate with embarrassing questions—to report back to Dan Evans himself on what transpired. It was obvious that the work exhilarated Ted, both the status and the subterfuge.

He was so animated in his account that it gave me an idea. I'd recently bought a cassette player with a built in microphone capable of recording audio. While he spoke, I pulled out my new tape-recorder, excited to have an opportunity to put it to use.

As I aimed the device towards Ted, I could see his eyes sparkle. Far from protesting, far from clamming up, he hammed it up, loving the recognition. He seemed to savor the attention, the idea that what he said was being recorded.

Even then, I got the impression that Ted was holding court, and we—his awestruck audience—gathered around to hear tales of his exploits.

Later during his trial, with cameras and press following his every move, I'd see this animation emerge in Ted again, that same sparkle in his eyes. It seemed the reason for the attention didn't matter—Ted Bundy loved the spotlight.

\* \* \*

In September of 1973, a group of us huddled in our small front room around the little black and white television and watched Billie Jean King play Bobby Riggs in their infamous one-on-one tennis match.

The group was mostly women, but a couple guys—including Don— were in attendance. Every last one of us rooted for Billie Jean King.

She moved around the court with such agility and confidence, meeting each of Riggs's legendary lobs, attuned to her opponent's location, his footing, the way he held his racket, so she could find any weakness and exploit it. She almost seemed to be controlling him, sending him running around the court. I'd never seen anything like it.

When she won, everyone in the room went wild, especially the women. We didn't have to put it into words. We knew this represented something much bigger than a tennis match.

Things were changing all around.

A lot of men didn't like it.

\* \* \*

That year I got a job working at Pilgrim's Pantry, a themed restaurant that had the benefit of sitting directly next door to the back side of my apartment building. The owner was a neat, lean man who struggled to manage the still new business and his staff of mostly students.

He also drank. I don't know how much was the drinking and how much was sheer exhaustion, but I remember many afternoons arriving to open the restaurant only to find him passed out in one of the booths. We'd politely wake him, then we'd turn over the "Open" sign and unlock the door, and he'd carry on through the dinner rush seemingly unim- paired, business as usual.

The ambiance in the restaurant was what I'd imagine of a country inn in early New England. The dining room showcased a wall of giant, arched brick ovens where turkeys turned continuously on spits. Along with turkey, we served mashed potatoes, homemade pies, and the best apple dumplings in town, as if every day was Thanksgiving. It was an idealized portrait of Colonial America.

But Puritan it was not. All the servers were women, and we were required to wear pilgrim-themed uniforms: chunky high-heeled shoes with buckles and dresses with crisscross lace across the bodice. If a woman had any curves at all, the bodice would accentuate them.

Much to the notice of our customers.

Harassment was a common grievance amongst us, and we tried to support each other against the daily onslaught. I have to admit, the uniform didn't fit me like my other co-workers. I was small and skinny without a lot of curves to boast, so for me the bodice pretty easily laced all the way to the top. This, unfortunately, didn't make me immune from harassment.

I remember one instance in particular. I was lugging hot, heavy, earthenware plates of food to one of my tables, and my arms were completely full. As I approached, one of the male diners saw my occupied arms as an opportunity. He made some off-color comment about my chest, then he reached up to my bodice to untie the laces.

"If you don't stop, this entire meal is going in your lap," I said. He must have seen that I meant it, because his hand instantly retracted.

I set down the plates and smiled, always the professional. "I'm coming with your coffee next, and that could really do some damage, so you better not try it again."

He didn't. In fact, he left behind a very good tip.

Despite the fact that the restaurant was so close to my apartment, I still didn't like walking home alone. There'd been rumors of a stalker in the area, and after a shift dodging unwanted leers and advances, the thought that someone could be lurking in the shadows didn't seem like a stretch.

I decided the convenience of the location wasn't worth it. I quit.

❊ ❊ ❊

Two blocks in the other direction was a nondescript apartment I passed occasionally when running errands in the U-District. I couldn't say what it looked like—I never looked at it twice. I don't remember it ever being featured on the news or in any campus bulletin.

During the same time period that Ted was dropping by my place with groceries and regaling us with stories of his exploits, a woman named Karen Sparks Epley was brutally attacked inside her own bedroom in that nondescript apartment two blocks away. She was beaten with a metal rod so severely, the blows to her head caused significant vision and hearing loss. Then she was sexually assaulted in the same violent manner, causing internal damage and actually splitting her bladder. Somehow, she survived.

We lived so close to one another. We went to the same university. We easily could have been friends.

Instead no one told us a crime had taken place. No one alerted students living in the area that a violent incident had occurred right in the neighborhood. Aside from the hazy rumors about a possible stalker, we had no idea.

The truth is, I didn't even know about Karen for decades.

It was my cousin Ted who did those things to her.

The thought still makes me sick.

* * *

It was around this time that Ted stopped by and suggested we go out dancing. This was probably a Thursday night, since Don was still in Tacoma, and he typically spent weekends with me in Seattle.

We took Ted's Volkswagen Beetle. He drove us to Shilshole Bay Marina, to a place on the waterfront called the Windjammer.

Like usual, Ted was dressed conservatively with a button-down shirt, whereas I was sporting my best "poor-student chic" look in low-riding, flared jeans and a cute top. As we entered, I remember feeling jazzed and loose, excited to dance.

The air was that living, breathing kind of warm that can only come from body heat, and the dancefloor was heaving with couples bouncing and gyrating to the latest hits of the seventies, played good and loud. I began dancing immediately, but Ted led us farther onto the dancefloor, where he found a spot and pretty much stayed in it. He'd sort of move stiffly to the music, but his attention wasn't on dancing.

He scoured the room, surveying the other dancers.

I saw his stiffness as a challenge, one I happily accepted. As the music picked up, I got more and more into dancing, trying to goad him to look at me and shake out of it. But Ted wasn't interested. He continued watching the crowd.

Pretty soon I began to dance circles around him, trying to get his attention, trying to get him to loosen up and engage. No dice. He couldn't find the rhythm. He was clearly distracted.

The couple next to us threw me some smiles and opened ranks, so I could dance with them for a while. I moved between them and Ted, still trying to break through his shell. I'd wave my hand in front of his eyes, and he'd give me a big smile, but his attention was fleeting. Quickly the smile would disappear, and his hunting eyes would return to the room.

*What's he looking for?* I asked myself.

What was he looking for?

*Map by Garrett Greer and Rohan Beal*

# Missing Person

In 1974, I moved from Carter Hall Apartments to live with a grade school friend in a creaky old craftsman just off Aurora Avenue. The house, with its brick porch and lipstick-burgundy trim, was set on a hill from the street where it overlooked traffic with the tired elegance of an earlier era. It was a lovely little house whose memory transcends beyond the short period of time I actually lived there.

This is, in part, the trouble.

My roommate and I rented the ground floor, which we shared with her dog and another girl who lived upstairs. It wasn't unusual for all of us to congregate downstairs in the furnace-warmed front room after a long day, and though we all had our own jobs and boyfriends and lives, we felt an awful lot like a family.

One cold evening early in the year, my roommate had plans to grab dinner with a former roommate of hers, Lynda. Sprawled on the couch, I lazily watched as she piled on her coat and scarf. The winter sun had made its exit hours ago, and it was already dark. I wished her a good-night, then I settled in for a quiet night of television at home.

It felt like she'd barely been gone when the door opened again, air from outside nipping at my bare arms and ankles. Not even an hour had passed. Removing her coat, it's the look on my roommate's face that I remember most, knotted up with confusion.

"That was fast," I said.

"She never showed," was her baffled response.

This is how I remembered learning that Lynda Ann Healy had disappeared.

\* \* \*

When the Bundys would visit us at our cabin in Longbranch, we'd often head down to the beach. Growing up, Ted loved to explore the shoreline. As the tide drained out of the bay, it would leave little rivulets that we could walk up once we made it through the mud. Low tide revealed all kinds of sea life, a wonderland of colors and textures to discover. Starfish, sea anemones, oysters, clams, geoducks, mussels hanging off the pilings, little fingerling fish caught in the tide pools...so many magical creatures to *ooh* and *aah* over.

Low tide also brought stately herons walking along the tide pools, looking for a quick meal, while seagulls and other birds circled above, scoping out the buffet below. Sometimes I'd tear off a piece of bread from my lunch and toss it. As if a conjuring trick, a hundred gulls would appear out of nowhere.

I loved collecting on these excursions. The prettiest rocks, the biggest shells. I'd scour the bay for treasures delivered by the tides. To this day, I still keep them in my house.

Part of our beach was covered in oysters. At low tide, John and I kept oyster knives tucked in our waistbands. If we felt like it, we'd shuck one and eat it raw right on the beach. Walking out to the water's edge, we'd sometimes get squirted by thin streams of water, shot by clams through tiny holes in the mud. That was our cue to pull out shovels and dig them up for a clambake after letting them spit in buckets of sea water.

But through it all, we had to keep a careful eye on the tide. The turn would happen fast, water flooding the bay, leaving us scrambling for footing. We'd have to race back to safety or be left stranded, surrounded by the water that buried the land of enchantment we'd been exploring only moments earlier.

Here one second, gone the next.

Always changing. Always interesting.

With each tide, new discoveries were revealed, while other old ones were swept back out to sea or buried, lost.

Memories, I've found, are like the tides.

\* \* \*

If that house off Aurora Avenue had a personality, it would be a favorite old aunt—a little behind the times but warm and inviting. Its hospitality extended to all visitors, and our front room often became the unofficial site for gatherings.

They were rarely planned. Friends hardly knew they were staying until they realized they'd taken off their shoes and found a seat on one of the couches. The scratches and scuffs in the interior's mahogany trim bore happy testimony of visitors through the ages. We as hosts had little say. Before we knew it, our home was buzzing with laughter and chatter, a record playing in the background. We could only sit back and join in.

When Ted dropped by, he was an easy guest. Though he was there because of me, I never had to worry about taking care of him. He'd chime into conversations and was easily engaging. Ted was a good talker with a studied vocabulary, but he was an even better listener, nodding and giving the speaker his full attention. He still had that rare gift of making the subject of his attention feel like the only person in the world.

Even when we had others over, I never minded when Ted stopped by. In fact, I loved it. Ted was always a hit with our friends, and I was proud to be related to him.

*I was proud to be related to him.*

An old memory washed in by the tide.

✳ ✳ ✳

Though I've wracked my brain, I don't remember a specific instance that Ted and Lynda were ever at the house at the same time. I'd met Lynda through my roommate, but did she ever come over to visit when Ted was at the house? I know I never introduced them or saw the two of them meet.

However, I suppose they didn't even need to interact for the connection to be made. Through the years, I introduced Ted to plenty of other friends, women who could have easily fit his visual profile. But he never bothered my friends. It's my belief that he tried not to see his victims as actual people. I assume this made it easier on him for what he planned to do.

Years later, after the horrible truth came out, a girlfriend told me she was convinced the reason she was safe from Ted was precisely because she was my friend. She didn't say this with any degree of comfort, nor did I receive it with anything like pride.

Instead what we shared in that moment—I suppose what we'll always share—is guilt.

So after Lynda's skull was found on Taylor Mountain at one of Ted's proven "dump sites," I was left to fret. *Had he stopped by some night when Lynda was over visiting? Had Ted seen her for the first time at my house?*

*Was their connection because of me?*

This is the possibility that's haunted me most of my life.

\* \* \*

It goes without saying that there's been a staggering amount of material put into the world about Ted. With this book, I've added a little more. I don't quite know how I feel about that.

Until very recently, I've avoided all of it—at least all I possibly could. It's shocking how much he's become a part of the vernacular, a throw-away pop-culture reference or an answer on a Sunday crossword. Each mention of his name feels like an electric jolt straight to my nervous system. A shock of pain. So I've built a protective wall and made it thicker over the years, a conscious choice to remain naive.

It wasn't until I began thinking about telling my story that, in the name of research, I knew I needed to peek over and finally see what's on the other side.

I wonder if the writers of the books and the makers of the movies think of people like me, we family members, sitting down to crack open the dust jackets or navigate the television screen to whatever sensational title they've chosen.

I knew I couldn't do it just before bed or anytime after dark. Since I usually get up before Don, padding in my socks through the house as the sky slowly brightens, this quiet hour is often my most productive time of the day. With this in mind, I figured why not bite the bullet and watch a gruesome docuseries at seven in the morning?

With the early Washington sunlight just starting to glow through the windows, I wrapped myself up in a blanket, grabbed a notepad and pen, and I pushed play.

There was so much footage of Ted.

His face, his voice—this was the Ted that I remembered and yet not him at all. That confrontation alone, after all those years, was almost overwhelming. Perhaps for the first time I was seeing him as a known figure, a face commandeered by the general public so that traces I still caught—at certain angles and in certain lighting—of my own family resemblance felt deeply personal and jarring.

It didn't take long before the narrative came to Lynda's disappearance. I'd never seen many of the images—of the house where she was taken, the stunned roommates who'd been sleeping just upstairs—and they brought on a wave of emotions. I was transported back to 1974, feeling again the sickness we all felt.

As a timeline filled the screen, my mind started racing.

There are bins in my basement where I keep the things I've saved from my parents (my letters from Ted are kept in a completely separate room—I don't want them to defile the others). Inside these bins are all the letters my parents wrote to me after I left Arkansas to move back to Seattle.

With my mind still racing, I pulled out the bins and began thumbing through the envelopes. I didn't even open them. All I needed to check were the dates and mailing addresses.

Lynda disappeared in the early hours of February 1, 1974. According to the addresses where my parents were sending me mail, at that time I was still living in my Carter Hall apartment. I didn't move out until after I graduated a few months later.

Seeking a second opinion, I cornered Don as soon as he was up and asked if that timing sounded right to him. He agreed. He'd hauled most of my boxes up the stairs to the house, he reminded me. It left an impression.

All of this meant that when Lynda disappeared, I hadn't moved into the house off Aurora Avenue yet.

My head spun. The memory of that night, my roommate returning home early, that confused look on her face.

*She never showed.*

Had that not happened?

Had I just imagined it all?

Already the image in my mind began slipping, colors running, pooling.

I couldn't believe it.

Even though we weren't living together yet, that roommate was a childhood friend of mine, and she had previously lived with Lynda. I know the two of them remained friends. Maybe she'd told me about the thwarted dinner plans later, and over time I skewed my place in the story. Or maybe she never had plans to meet with Lynda at all.

I couldn't remember anymore.

The tide was washing it all away.

I did the only thing I could think to do. I contacted my old roommate and asked if we could meet. I had to find out what she remembered.

❊ ❊ ❊

She didn't want to talk about it.

I understand.

How could I not? Until very recently, it's exactly how I've felt. We all have different journeys, different needs, and I can't respect hers enough.

When I left the house to meet with her, I printed off a list of questions, so I wouldn't forget everything I wanted to ask.

*Did she have plans to meet up with Lynda when she disappeared?*

*After I moved in with her, does she remember Ted coming by the house? What did she think of him at the time?*

*What was it like for her when she found out the identity of the man who had committed the crimes?*

*Did that change how she felt about me?*

This paper remained folded inside my pocket. I never took it out.

Now, I suppose, I'll have the list forever. These unanswered questions.

❊ ❊ ❊

But even as that particular section in my timeline has gone underwater, one point has been washed, clean, to the surface.

If I didn't live in the house off Aurora before Lynda went missing, then Ted hadn't visited me there yet.

In other words, there's no way he met Lynda at my house.

The connection between them hadn't come through me, an unwitting executioner.

For decades I'd hung onto this guilt. This simmering worry.

It isn't lost on me that I could have resolved this long ago if only I hadn't closed myself off so entirely. The information was easily attainable. A cursory internet search could have given me a timeline. My reluctance to deal with my hurt became its own hurt, which I've held onto for years.

Now, I suppose I can finally let that go with the tides.

# Letter from Edna to Ted in Prison

*Written after getting no response to her last letter,
as Ted's execution date approached.*

*Transcription of entire letter.*

June 10, 1986

Dear Ted,

Once again I feel that it is important for me to encourage you to make a very important decision...perhaps one of the most important decisions of your life. I am strongly urging you to tell the whole story. Ted, you have a date with the executioner. My God, your time is terribly short. You are going to die. But, one thing you can do is tell people why you did it. Tell people, Ted, why you murdered their daughters and where you left their bodies. There are many anguished families who have a right to know. None of them did anything to you. They were not responsible for your past. As I said before, I will come to Florida if you want to talk to me about it. But, cutting out the lies would make a big impression on a lot of people. In fact, if you had the guts to tell the whole story you'd get a tremendous amount of media coverage. If there is a heaven or a hell— maybe this would make a difference for you in eternity.

Ted, everyone knows you committed these crimes. As a matter of fact I am personally really tired of you trying to cover up for them. So you got lots of attention for doing it...That's just great. You sure chose a God awful way to get even or whatever your mind grasped onto to justify your acts. By the way, Ted, how did you (and how do you) justify murder? Did you say...Well, these girls deserved it because they came on to me? I'd like to know what it was that made you cross the line. Or did it really start much sooner than anyone knows? Did you start off killing paper girls in your spare time to practice or what?

Ted, so many years I denied the evidence. I stuck by you—I loved you like a brother. I ran across an old cassette tape that I made when I lived in my apartment in the U district. There is so much affection in our voices when we spoke to each other. I really loved you so much Ted. I wouldn't be writing a letter like this if I didn't think that maybe I still have some influence on you. Ted, it would mean so much to so many people if you would drop the pretense. Could you do it? Are you too scared about dying to make decisions...or are you relieved that the end is near? Either way, what do you think of my proposition?

Your cousin,

Edna

P.S. Did you get my last letter (2 weeks ago)?

June 10, 1986

Dear Ted,

Once again I feel that it is important for me to encourage you to make a very important decision... perhaps one of the most important decisions of your life. I am strongly urging you to tell the whole story. Ted, you have a date with the executioner. My God, your time is terribly short. You are going to die. But, one thing you can do is tell people why you did it. Tell people, Ted, why you murdered their daughters and where you left their bodies. There are many anguished families who have a right to know. None of them did anything to you. They were not responsible for your past. As I said before, I will come to Florida if you want to talk to me about it. But, cutting out the lie could make a big impression on a lot of people. In fact, if you had the guts to tell the whole story you'd get a tremendous amount of media coverage. If there is a heaven or a hell — maybe this would make a difference for you in eternity.

Ted, everyone knows you committed these crimes. As a matter of fact I am personally really tired of you trying to cover up

**ROBERT D. KEPPEL**
*DETECTIVE*

344 -7563
344-8997
344-3883

DEPARTMENT OF PUBLIC SAFETY
KING COUNTY COURTHOUSE
SEATTLE, WASHINGTON 98104

# Spree

It's hard to describe the fear that swept the Seattle area. By the summer of 1974, it grew clear that something big was happening. I believe it began really taking shape around the time Georgann Hawkins disappeared.

Lynda had been missing by then for over four months. The winter ski forecasts, which Lynda used to report on the radio, had disappeared along with the snow. Spring came and went. And still Lynda was just...gone. My friends and I anxiously combed the papers as the days turned to weeks, weeks to months, but there was never any news. Our simmering unease boiled into foreboding. *What had happened to her?* We lost hope for a positive outcome, some innocent misunderstanding that could easily resolve, where life could simply pick up again where it left off. The truth likely wasn't good, but we needed to know. Openly, the police admitted they had no leads.

I've learned, from a police report now made public, that on June 8, 1974, I apparently had dinner with Ted and John as well as the roommate who'd taken over Margie's spot at my Carter Hall apartment. This was a regular occurrence, and I can only assume Ted acted completely normally, because I can't remember the occasion at all.

Two days later, in an attempt to push the stalled investigation forward, Lynda's parents began offering a reward. On June 10, 1974, a notice in the *Seattle Times* reported that they'd give $1,000 for "information leading to a safe return" of their daughter. That very night, in the early hours of June 11, Georgann Hawkins vanished.

I remember when it hit the news. After all the papers I'd bought and searched page by page, I'm not sure what sort of development I'd been expecting. But this certainly wasn't it.

Georgann, like Lynda, was a student at the University of Washington and disappeared from the U-District. The similarities between the two women were impossible to brush aside. And moreover, the possibility of a link triggered the notion of a larger pattern. Police began reconsidering other recent missing person cases for signs that they might fit, too.

At this time, I was twenty-two years old, a recent graduate from UW, and living just a few miles from where Lynda and Georgann had been abducted. The foreboding I'd felt in regards to Lynda now turned to outright terror. And it wasn't just me who felt it.

Back then there were about six television channels: four, five, seven, nine, eleven, and thirteen, if I remember correctly. This meant everyone watched essentially the same thing, be it *All in the Family* or the evening news. When the reports started to break that police were investigating a potential pattern of missing college-aged women, the community learned about it together.

We didn't have the vocabulary then to discuss "serial killers." The term didn't yet exist as a part of public discourse, and without a way to talk about it, there was really no awareness. So the idea that someone might be hunting women our age who looked an awful lot like us, stealing them away from the very streets where we lived....

It changed everything.

We stopped going out at night. The weather turned hot and sticky, but no one dared open a window. Nobody had air conditioning in Seattle in those days, yet house after house, apartment after apartment stayed shut up tight that summer, the women inside climbing the walls, stewing in sweat and fear.

Hitchhiking had been very common. The entrance ramps to I-5 by UW were often crowded with young men and women, thumbs sticking out. Without a car, I sometimes hitchhiked myself, once going all the way to Tacoma. As word of the disappearances got out, hitchhiking in the city practically came to a halt overnight. Don, who lived in Tacoma at the time, begged me never to do it again, but he didn't need to beg. I was done forever. Aside from the bus to and from work, my ten-speed bike became my primary means of transport. But even on that I felt vulnerable, my eyes scanning each new block for threats, carefully avoiding routes that were isolated. At least it was safer than walking.

No matter our precautions, the fear followed us like a presence. Everyday life—grocery shopping, going to work, getting a haircut—felt elevated and dangerous. The collective resting heart rate that summer undoubtedly rose a few beats.

\* \* \*

Unbelievably this wasn't the only worry that dogged us. It was the mid-seventies, and the U.S. was back in a recession. The country was struggling to find its footing from the oil crisis that resulted in blocks-long lines at the gas pumps (I remember several altercations when people tried to cut), the Vietnam War from which many soldiers were returning, a steep decline in jobs, and the Watergate scandal that would soon push Richard Nixon out of office. The resulting brew of unrest and uncertainty made for an economy that was trying—and so far, failing—to find equilibrium. Devastating unemployment was coupled with inflation exceeding 11 percent and high interest rates of 9 percent, a combination that economists hadn't even thought possible. Things were so bad, the term "stagflation" was coined to describe it, and it was going to get a lot worse.

It was, in short, a terrible time to graduate—with a BA in History to top it off. Like most of my fellow graduates, I struggled to find meaningful—or any—work. Forget career paths forged from our college degrees, my friends and I were grateful for any job that paid the rent.

So it was with no other options that for over a year after graduation, I worked the front desk for an orthodontist in downtown Seattle at the Medical Dental Building. Though I needed the job, it was not a good fit. I wish I could say it paid well. I remember when I got my first paycheck. I took one look at the amount and wondered to myself if it was worth the effort of going across the street to the bank to deposit it.

But it wasn't the pay or even the work itself that made the job so miserable, though I chafed at doing something more challenging. The poison in that office ran deeper.

The doctor there was a very well-respected orthodontist and passionate about what he did. More than twenty years my senior, I saw him as something of a fatherly figure, so I wasn't on my guard when he invited me to join him as he looked at some patient x-rays.

Thinking this was a part of my training, I stood next to him and carefully examined the slides as he pointed out various points of interest, not clocking just how close he'd gotten. When his hand rested on the small of my back, I didn't know what to think.

Don't get me wrong, this wasn't the first time I'd been the target of a pass. There were many instances during parties at Far-A-Way in which I'd been forced to rebuff the advances of drunk men. But the doctor wasn't drunk. In fact, he was my boss. And I really needed that job.

Hoping to avoid an uncomfortable scene, I discreetly tried to move away, but I found it difficult in such a small space. Thankfully there was a knock at the door, and one of my co-workers walked in with a question for the doctor. She stopped short as his hand darted away from my back.

My relief cannot be overstated. She'd saved me. And more than that, she'd witnessed what had happened. I was sure I could count on her as my ally if I needed backup for any potential incident in the future.

I was wrong.

Ultimately, the doctor didn't end up being much of a problem. He made a few more quiet advances, which I was very quick to refuse, and he actually took the hint.

My co-worker, however, made my job a living hell. She quickly spread gossip around the office that I was trying to seduce the doctor, and outside of a couple friends, everyone was happy to believe her. I learned the hard way that a rumor in an office is like a steak in a lion's den. Once introduced, there's no force on earth strong enough to wrench it back out. And if you try, you face the claws.

I was forced to accept that there was nothing I could do. I'd been shut out. My shunning wasn't even confined to our office alone. Several dental practices in the building funneled into one employee break room for lunch. On multiple occasions, I remember walking in and everyone instantly stopped talking. Each day was a different shade of awful, and I dreaded going to work.

But going home to the fear of an unknown killer was worse.

❄ ❄ ❄

During this tense time, it was a welcome reprieve whenever Ted stopped by the house off Aurora Avenue to visit.

On one hot afternoon, some other friends were over, and someone had had the good idea to bring some weed. Considering all that was going on, we welcomed the opportunity to blow off some steam.

As we sat around the living room, passing a doobie and listening to a record, my roommate's dog alerted us that another visitor was approaching the house.

It was Ted.

As he joined us in the living room, Ted was quickly offered the joint. Smiling, he refused, and the rest of us continued to smoke while we all talked.

After a few minutes, I stepped into the kitchen to grab drinks for the group. When I turned back, I was surprised to find that Ted had followed me into the room.

He clearly had something on his mind. It seemed important to him to tell me that he didn't want to smoke pot because he feared "losing control," and I was reminded of his aversion to risk-taking games as a kid. Inwardly I thought his concerns were a little dramatic, but I told him he didn't have to do anything he didn't want to. Hoping to have put his mind at ease, we both returned to the others in the living room.

Whatever had been going through his head, I have no idea, but when the joint passed his direction again, this time he took it.

After only a few puffs, the transformation was dramatic.

At first, I admit it was fun. Ted was always wound a bit tight, and it seemed like he could do with some loosening. But once he got stoned, Ted became wild and loud.

The record was still playing in the background, and Ted began to dance. Swept up in a party spirit, others joined in, but I couldn't take my eyes off Ted. I had never seen him move like that before. Weed usually mellows people out, but Ted's movements grew spasmodic and agitated. *Whoa man*, I remember thinking. *Chill out. Who is this guy? Because he sure isn't acting like my cousin.* As the others began to register that something was slightly off, Ted jumped up on the coffee table and continued to dance.

By then, no one else was dancing. We all watched Ted, unsure if what was occurring was harmless fun or if someone needed to intervene before he hurt himself.

It didn't take long for Ted to snap out of it. Almost sheepishly, he stepped off the coffee table and returned to his seat.

He didn't touch the joint again.

Afterwards, I remember feeling embarrassed for Ted. I sensed that I'd gotten a glimpse behind his careful facade to a private sanctum he didn't like to reveal.

* * *

Though Ted freely dropped by my apartment, I never visited him at the boarding house where he rented a room, even though it was only a short distance away. There were only a couple of times that I did stop by briefly as a meet-up spot before we set off for other plans, but I was never invited inside. On only one occasion, I came unannounced.

I remember Ted looked harried when he came to the door. Instead of asking me in, he suggested we go someplace else.

"You'd better not come in," he said. "It's a real mess in there."

I assured him I didn't care. I'd grown up with a brother. Surely I'd seen it all.

He almost looked like he was considering it, but he admitted he was too embarrassed. "I really don't want you to see this."

Then he left me out on the front step while he went back inside to grab his things.

*This is weird*, I remember thinking. *He must really not want me to see what a slob he is.* Considering Ted's usual preppy, composed demeanor, it sort of made sense. Appearances meant a lot to Ted. Similar to his experience getting stoned at my apartment, I figured he didn't want to let me peek behind the curtain.

John, who hung out with Ted frequently, told me years later that he was never invited into Ted's apartment either, and there was only one instance that he got a glimpse inside. It was just a fleeting look before Ted blocked him out.

In that moment, John's eyes landed on some very expensive ski gear and stereo equipment—multiple pairs of Head brand skis and high-end amps stacked on top of each other. This didn't make sense to John, who knew that Ted was currently between paying jobs and struggling for money. John remembered thinking, *Where did that come from?* Had Ted traded for it? Was he storing it for a friend?

He asked Ted about the costly gear, but Ted brushed it off as nothing and expertly steered the conversation to other topics. John didn't think about it again until years later, after Ted was arrested in Utah, when details began emerging that Ted had a history of theft.

Is that what he was hiding from me?

Or was it much worse?

Later, reports said that Ted sometimes dismembered the bodies of the women he'd killed and brought back souvenirs—usually their severed heads—to his rooming house.

I think about myself standing out on the step that day, thinking my cousin was being silly for not inviting me in.

What would I have seen?

＊ ＊ ＊

As the summer wore on, edgier and stickier with each passing day, we learned that authorities were formally coordinating the search efforts among a number of missing person cases, in the belief that they were in fact the work of the same person. Then, there in print with pictures attached, we were given a list of names.

Lynda Ann Healy, last seen January 31. Donna Gail Manson, March 12. Susan Elaine Rancourt, April 17. Georgann Hawkins, June 11. Later others were included. A woman in Oregon named Roberta Kathleen Parks, missing since May 6. And Brenda Carol Ball, last seen in Burien on May 31.

During this time of confusion, information came out so furiously, with authorities still investigating and ironing out facts, that the list wasn't clear cut. At times other names were included only to be removed when the woman was either found alive or, unfortunately more often, discovered to have been killed in an unrelated matter.

But with the names in front of us, one after another, our horror took on a shape. We could imagine these women as they must have been—daughters, friends, lovers—and feel the pang of their absence to families who would never be the same. *That could've been me*, we thought. Then, looking at their photos: *That practically is me.*

It was with this in mind that my brother, John, showed up at the house early one evening with Ted by his side. My housemates hadn't arrived home yet, and I had the place to myself. As I welcomed in my unexpected guests, I noticed John was carrying a bag from the hardware store.

"What's that?" I asked, and John explained that, with all the abductions going on, he didn't trust the locks on our doors. He proceeded to pull out two brand-new surface-mounted barrel bolts, and he asked if he could borrow a screwdriver.

As John went about installing the extra locks, locks meant to keep out the dangerous criminal preying on women in the region, Ted and I watched and chatted with him idly.

I don't remember the conversation or how long they stayed. Nothing about this occasion felt memorable at the time. I vaguely recall, though, that Ted amiably teased John's handiwork and offered some tips on the installation.

He always liked to be helpful.

It chills me, how effectively Ted had masked himself from us, and that evening we picked up no threatening vibes. No subliminal messages or warnings remotely made it through. Yet here was the man who would be labeled one of the most dangerous serial killers in the world, casually doling out advice and instruction to install locks meant to protect us against him.

The lock was installed, the bolt secured. Ted stood right there next to us, already inside. But it didn't matter anyway. Ted could have come in anytime he wanted. He just had to knock.

❊ ❊ ❊

On July 14, Janice Ott and Denise Naslund vanished from a busy park near Lake Sammamish. I vividly remember watching the newscasts, curled up on the sofa, strained tight with dread. In the reports, police tried to assure the public that these disappearances may not be connected to the other missing women. Lake Sammamish was different, they said in interviews. The two incidents occurred in the middle of the day, on the same day, and in a crowded place.

Even still, the cases never really felt separate to me, despite the cautions we were given. Somewhere in the stories about Denise and Janice, the names of the other women would be mentioned, drawing the inevitable connection.

It came as no surprise, then, when the reports quickly dropped the pretense of separation and simply began covering the similarities: age range, background, appearance. There was an important difference, though, that had occurred that day at Lake Sammamish. The man believed to be responsible had been observed by several witnesses.

\* \* \*

When the details were released, I rushed to the newsstand and bought a copy of the *Seattle Post-Intelligencer*. The story filled the front page, where a name jumped out from the print. According to multiple witnesses, the man last seen with each woman had introduced himself as "Ted."

Ted was not an uncommon name. And moreover, it seemed highly unlikely that the man had had the audacity to use his real name. The pseudonym, surely, had to be random.

He'd driven, said multiple witnesses, a Volkswagen Beetle.

Okay that was a strange coincidence. My cousin Ted drove a Beetle.

But it was the mid-seventies. Beetles were one of the most popular car models around—tens of thousands were registered in the state of Washington alone. No less than four of Don's friends drove Beetles. The streets and parking lots were well and truly infested with Bugs.

I searched the report for more details. Witnesses at the park had remembered the car as brown, or even "metallic brown."

Ted's VW was tan. Light tan, a few shades off ivory. Could some people describe it as brown?

I called Don to tell him what I'd read.

And we laughed.

We agreed it was simply too unimaginable to consider. There was no way my cousin Ted was the guy police were looking for. It's difficult to understand now, with all that came out later, but at the time it felt like pure coincidence. An amusing fluke. Our instinctual response was not "oh, that's concerning," but instead "oh, that's funny."

After all, none of the other facts fit.

Most prominently, the article showed a composite sketch that had been drawn to look like the man witnesses remembered. To Don and me, this sketch looked absolutely nothing like Ted.

Moreover, at the park "Ted" was described as having a slight English accent and had his arm in a sling, which, according to witness reports, was why he asked the women for help unloading a small sailboat from his car. My cousin had never been to England, had no arm injuries or broken bones, and definitely didn't own a sailboat. I wasn't sure he even knew how to sail.

No, the name and the car were just a fluke. Nothing significant, easily dismissed. We'd never have thought about the connection again except, of course, that we knew we couldn't waste the opportunity to tease Ted about it the next time we saw him.

Lucky for us, we didn't have to wait long.

\* \* \*

It was evening when Ted next stopped by the house. I believe it was Friday, as Don had driven up from Tacoma for the weekend. The copy of the *Seattle Post-Intelligencer* was still sitting on the table, and I opened it to show to Ted.

Grinning, Don pointed to the police sketch. "Ted, wow, that looks just like you."

A good sport, Ted smiled.

I watched, amused, as Don pointed out that the suspect had gone by the name "Ted" and reportedly drove a Volkswagen, a fact he punctuated by gesturing out the window to Ted's own car parked out front.

"You don't happen to have a phony sling you like to wear sometimes, do you? How about a secret sailboat?" Don teased. "Or anything else you'd like to confess?"

Ted threw back his head to laugh. "As a matter of fact," he said, "the police have been in contact with me."

The grins dropped from our faces. *What?*

Ted went on to explain that he'd received a call from the police department as part of their routine checks. They'd acquired a list of all Volkswagens in the state with owners named Ted, a list of "four-hundred guys," he said (a number I later learned he'd inflated). Ted had answered a few simple questions, to which the officer seemed satisfied, and that was that. He explained it all nonchalantly, as if casually interested at this peek into the inner workings of the justice system.

Don and I were blown away. He'd really been contacted by the police? We actually felt sorry for him, that he'd been inconvenienced over this random stroke of bad luck. "Not you, Ted," Don said, incredulous that someone like Ted could be caught up in a criminal investigation.

But Ted assured us it was fine. The police, he said, were only doing their job.

\* \* \*

I can recall only one instance when not everyone was so easily fooled by Ted.

In our rented house off Aurora Avenue, my roommate and I shared the ground floor with her dog, Jeffy. Jeffy was an adorable mutt, medium sized, and bursting with the energy of a younger and smaller dog. Find a human to throw a ball for him, and Jeffy was living like a king. As it happened, Jeffy was also a great watchdog, making him an even more valuable member of the household. No one could approach the house without us knowing it.

In those days it was commonplace for friends to stop by, planned or not, just to say hello. Thanks to Jeffy, we always knew someone was coming before they reached the door. It went like this: Jeffy would start barking, prompting us to look out the window, where we'd discern the identity of our guest based on the vehicle parked down on the curb. Once we'd assured Jeffy it was okay and invited the visitor inside, Jeffy would still take it on himself to ascertain that there was no danger. Once satisfied, he'd immediately calm down, back to his regular, playful self, and demand love and ear-rubs from the guest he'd accosted only seconds earlier.

On one particular day, my roommate and I were both home when Jeffy began barking. I ran to the window and pulled back the curtains. Parked outside was Ted's familiar Volkswagen. The car was an occasional but always happy sight on our street. Delighted, I rushed to the door to let him inside.

This was far from the first time Jeffy had encountered Ted at the house. But on this occasion, even after I'd assured Jeffy all was well, the dog grew more agitated. As soon as Ted entered through the door, Jeffy lunged at him.

My roommate grabbed the dog by his collar, fighting to hold him back. Jeffy was in pure attack mode, fangs bared, hackles up, biting and snapping at Ted's ankles and pant legs. Ted sidestepped, dancing around the lunging animal as I helped my roommate restrain him.

We were shocked and apologetic, my roommate explaining to Ted that she'd never seen Jeffy do this before, but it was difficult to speak above the volume of his barking. Battling against his restraints, Jeffy reared up on his hind legs, now fully chest height, and tried again to lunge. It took both of us to hold him back.

Through all this, Ted behaved like a true gentleman. Between our shouted apologies and Jeffy's barking, he reassured us that it was alright. He must've stepped in something, he explained, or been around another dog and picked up its scent. That certainly was the reason for Jeffy's reaction. Nothing for us to feel badly about.

Despite our assurances, it was abundantly clear that Jeffy wasn't going to back down. Using all her strength, my roommate hauled the frenzied Jeffy to a back room. He did not go willingly, twisting and scratching, trying to wrench out of her grip. Finally she got him inside and managed to lock the door.

BAM! Instantly Jeffy began to throw himself at the door, still barking like mad. The door shuddered with each impact.

Again we apologized, and again Ted assured us it was fine. As the sound of scratching was punctuated by Jeffy's body slamming over and over against the door, we tried not to notice, more concerned with making sure Ted was okay. Meanwhile, Jeffy's desperate message to us was deliberately ignored.

That was the one and only time Jeffy acted like that. It was so out of character, my roommate told me years later that afterwards she never felt quite the same around Ted. I had no idea she felt that way.

Of course, I'll never know exactly why Jeffy had that reaction, or what Ted had been doing right before he came to the house. Anyone's guess is as good as mine.

I learned much later that Ted had certain locations in the mountains where he liked to dump the bodies of the women he'd killed, and that he liked to revisit those locations from time to time. This whole idea makes me physically ill. I have no clue if that's where he'd been. But when I remember Jeffy's reaction, his desperate lunges at Ted's ankles, it's a possibility that sticks with me.

\* \* \*

In August, Ted packed up and moved to Salt Lake City for law school. I was sad to see him go. It was only temporary, he assured us when he broke the news. His life was in Washington. He'd be back.

After August, news coverage in the Seattle area continued on the missing women and "Ted" as new leads were chased then eliminated, and later bones began to be discovered in the mountains. But no new names were added to the list.

We had no idea that in Utah another list had begun.

# The Space Between

I stepped farther into the shadows. *C'mon, John. Where is it?*
Since my brother's schedule meant he'd still be at work when I was set to arrive at his apartment, he said he'd hide the key for me in the overgrown space between the two buildings. He'd hang it from a string, he said. I wouldn't be able to miss it.

I was definitely missing it.

This would have been around July of 1975. Ted had been in Utah for nearly a year, and though we had no idea why, the series of brutal murders in the Seattle area had stopped. That didn't erase it from our minds—we'd never leave behind a certain vigilance verging on paranoia, primed in case it started up again—but the fever of the following year had cooled to a slightly less frenzied level. Despite the fact that we still had no answers, the community was trying hard to move on.

At this time, my brother, John, lived in the Lewis and Clark apartments in north Tacoma. Designed in 1909 to be the finest apartment building in the city, the Lewis came first, followed quickly by its twin, the Clark. They were, and still are, stately structures clad in red brick with timber-framed top stories. Surrounded by thick, old trees, they exude an old-world elegance.

They also represented my brother's home, a place where I felt comfortable. Perhaps this put me slightly off my guard.

After parking my '64 Ford Country Squire woody station wagon (a car I'd recently purchased and loved dearly) on the street, I rounded the thick bushes and headed directly to the empty gap between the buildings. Repeating John's instructions in my head, I cast my eyes around for the glint of a key hanging on a string.

Nothing.

*Okay*, I thought to myself. *It must have fallen.*

My attention turned downwards. This overgrown area wasn't meant for public use, and I had to focus in order to search, pushing aside branches and leaves, crouching around untamed bushes.

I was so intent on my task that I didn't notice that I was no longer alone until I heard the rustling of footsteps.

Turning quickly, I saw a man. He'd entered the alley from the back side of the building, coming from the parking lot. The look on his face made my blood freeze. There was a blackness in his eyes, a rigid set to his jaw that seemed distantly familiar, and it left no doubt of his intentions.

He was there to hurt me.

It wasn't until years later that I realized this was the same look I'd seen fall over Ted's face the night he danced with Margie in our small apartment, an image forever burned into my memory.

\* \* \*

It happened fast. Way too fast. By the time I'd straightened up and realized what was going on, he was already rushing at me.

I remember temporarily freezing. Why did I do that? It was only a fraction of a second, but why didn't I use that time to turn and run?

In truth, I know it wouldn't have made a difference. He came at me so fast that as I regained my wits, and I turned to beat feet, he'd already caught up to me.

WHAM! His fist pounded into the right side of my face. I'll forever remember the sound it made, loud and hard. I saw stars, felt disoriented but no pain. Not yet.

I remember the outrage and terror but also the denial. *No, please, this can't be it.* But before I could respond, he slugged me again. I knew I was in serious trouble, but it was all happening so fast. *He's trying to immobilize me,* I thought. *So that I can't fight back. So that he can....*

Before I even had time to comprehend the horrors of what lay ahead, the man had grabbed me by my arm, and he slammed me against the building. Instead of hitting the brick wall, my body flung into the basement window of a below-grade apartment. The glass shattered as my elbow smashed through it.

I'm so glad it did. The sound of the breaking glass spooked him. I could see it in his eyes, the animal-like tensing of his body. It had made too much noise. He was scared.

As quickly as he'd come, he took off running. I can still see the image of him fleeing away, retreating back from where he'd come.

Through it all I hadn't screamed, hadn't spoken a word, but at that moment I found my voice. Pulling myself from the broken shards of glass, I swear to God, I called after him,

"You should see someone and get help!"

❊ ❊ ❊

I suppose I should have stuck around and waited for the police, but I wasn't thinking straight. I was consumed with a terror that the man would come back. Nothing else mattered. I had to get the hell out of there.

Somehow, I carried myself back to my car. My hands were trembling so hard I could barely get the key into the lock to let myself in. Finally the door swung open, and I fell into the familiarity of the car's interior. Still in survival mode, I immediately checked the backseat to make sure it was empty. It was. I hurried to lock the doors, and that's when I noticed I was bleeding.

My right elbow was chewed up pretty badly where it had broken through the glass. Still in shock, I remember the disappointment that I was wearing one of my favorite shirts, now ruined from bloodstains.

Sitting there behind the wheel, shaking with adrenaline, I became flooded with a feeling of gratitude. *I was so lucky.* This could have easily, so, so easily, ended differently. Thank God I'd hit that window instead of the bricks. I can hardly bring myself to think what would have happened to me if I hadn't. Would I have been raped? Would I have been killed?

I was alive.

Perhaps inevitably, my mind raced to that list of women, those I'd seen over and over in the news.

Behind the scenes, detectives in Utah and Washington were just beginning to close in on Ted as a suspect, but nothing had been released to the public, so as far as we knew, the killer was still out there. Even still, I didn't believe this was the same guy. I don't know exactly why.

Maybe I was prescient, or maybe I was naive. But somehow I knew this wasn't him.

Yet still I couldn't help but experience an even deeper sensitivity for what those women must have felt. For the first (and only) time, I knew what it felt like to believe I was going to die. I knew violence. Danger. I knew paralyzing, present, urgent fear.

And wrapped inside it all hid a dark feeling of guilt. Of responsibility. *How could I have been so dumb*, I somehow thought amidst my torrent of emotions, *to have gone into a dark space alone? How could I have allowed myself to lose awareness of my surroundings while I focused on hunting for that damn key?* In the moments after being assaulted, I was actually blaming myself.

Did those women also feel that way? While they were dying, did they wrongly, terribly feel ashamed?

It's a symptom, I think, of an empathetic soul, very often shown in women. We absorb responsibility even when we shouldn't. And it's a characteristic Ted knew how to twist and manipulate. He'd put his arm in a sling and ask for help. The kindest of women were exactly the type to be reeled in.

It shatters me to think that, in their final moments before dying in the worst way I can imagine, they might have felt something like shame for their own goodness.

*❋ ❋ ❋*

Sitting in the safety of my own car, as tears streamed down my face, I felt that by surviving I'd been given a rare chance. I made a vow right there, on the spot. *This will not define me*, I promised myself. *This will not change the direction of my life.*

Fighting back nausea and sending a fervent prayer of thanks up into the heavens, I turned on the car.

*❋ ❋ ❋*

I don't remember deciding where to go. It's as if my trusty Ford wagon simply transported me there. In a blur, I arrived at the house of some friends, Max and Sonja, about ten minutes away. The sight of Max's car in the driveway filled me with relief.

Someone was home.

I made it to the front door just as it opened, and Max greeted me with a smile beaming across his face. The smile didn't last long. His gaze fell over me. My eye was starting to swell shut where I'd been slugged, and blood was running down my arm.

Immediately Max helped me into the house. With a new surge of emotion, I knew that I wasn't alone any longer. Here was someone I could lean on, someone who would help carry my load and get me through this. Somehow my eyes found new tears to shed.

Through the tears, I told Max what had happened, and he fought down his own anger and horror in order to stay level-headed. He insisted that he would drive me to the emergency room.

They put sixteen stitches in my elbow. By then, the adrenaline was wearing off, and I felt it. All of it. I hurt all over, and the fullness of my condition became more apparent with each tender movement, each stabbing wince. Thank goodness for the staff at the hospital who treated me with such kindness and concern.

By law, they had to notify the police, and we waited for an officer to arrive and interview me. Max stayed with me at the hospital through it all.

Afterwards he drove me back to his house, where he cooked us a pot of his infamously spicy chili while Sonja fed their two-month-old baby and fussed over me. God, that baby was the best distraction. Without his smiles and cries and eager curiosity at life around him, I'm afraid we all could have been swallowed up in horror.

Soon Don arrived, having rushed over as soon as he heard what had happened from John. As he wrapped me in his arms, I felt safe. With Don by my side, I was almost ready to believe I'd be able to keep the promise I made to myself.

I wouldn't let this define me.

✳ ✳ ✳

Later, Don told me how helpless he'd felt and angry at being rendered helpless. He was overcome with a desire to find the guy. He wanted, he admitted, to run him over with his truck.

Like me, Don felt an overwhelming sense of guilt. He felt, illogically, as if he should have prevented it from happening.

I didn't know this at the time, but in the months following my attack, Don went out driving around the north Tacoma neighborhood, looking for my assailant. He didn't know what he'd do if he found someone who fit my description. I have to say I'm glad he never did.

Don had been taught hand-to-hand combat in the Marine Corps, and if it'd come to a confrontation, I have no doubt who'd have won the fight.

Incidentally, we never learned if the guy was ever caught. I was told by the police, when they came to the house a few days later for a second interview, that I wasn't his only victim. In fact, they said, they believed he was escalating.

\* \* \*

Surviving a violent attack didn't make me feel strong. It made me realize how vulnerable I was. I vowed to become stronger as a result.

I went over the incident in my head countless times. I knew the attack wasn't my fault, but I grew determined to do everything in my power to safeguard against it happening again. Just as I'd done after Don's injurious experience skydiving, I reminded myself of the importance of being smart. Preparation, I believed, meant protection. I promised myself I'd never again lose awareness of my surroundings, no matter where I was, no matter how intent I became on my task at hand.

Would this have significantly changed anything that day? I'll never know. Later I found out that John had completely forgotten to hide the key, as we'd arranged. He felt so bad about it, he could barely utter the confession to me.

I knew it wasn't on purpose, and I could see he felt horrible, so I made the decision in that moment not to blame him.

Yet still, in my resolution to never again be caught unaware, I didn't like to think that I'd been there, vulnerable, in the space between the buildings, searching for nothing.

\* \* \*

Shortly after this experience, I signed a contract with Eastpoint Seafoods to travel to Dutch Harbor in Alaska and work on a processing ship through the Alaskan king crab season. I'd be leaving in September.

The job promised much better pay than I made at the orthodontist's, which I was keen to leave anyway, but there was more to my decision than that. Between the unsolved murders and then my own vicious attack, I was desperate to leave.

Seattle would always be my home, but at the moment it was killing me.

❊ ❊ ❊

*You should see someone and get help.*

Why did I say that to him? I still wonder.

I wasn't being snide or sarcastic. I was very sincere.

This was before we learned the truth about Ted, before the ground was wrenched out from underneath me. At that time, even as I was bruised and bleeding from this man's hands, it seemed clear I thought of my attacker as someone who could be redeemed.

I didn't know, then, that there are people who have no interest in redemption.

# Letter from Edna to Ted in Prison

*Written the day Ted was granted a stay of execution.*
*Stamped but never sent.*

*Transcription of entire unsent letter.*

July 2, 1986

Dear Ted,

I just heard that you've been granted an indefinite (is the right word stay?) of execution. I am glad.

Capital punishment is absolutely medieval. I have never believed that the government should have the right to murder someone.

Anyway, I wanted you to know that we are sighing with relief...at least for now. Ted, I don't want you to go to the electric chair—GOD!

I have written you some pretty strong letters lately. It doesn't change how I feel. We are all victims of this on a daily basis.

For example: This morning I was working with a photographer shooting the interior of a restaurant on Shilshole Bay. The models were all talking about your impending execution. It just tore me up thinking about it. These sorts of things happen constantly. You are notorious, cousin, there is no doubt about it.

My dad and I tried to call your mother last night...we wanted to let her know that we are still a family and we care. When she didn't answer we realized how stupid we were...of course she would be with you.

Ted, I know now that you are very reluctant to talk about the unsolved murders attributed to you. It would be extremely bold and risky. I guess if you admit to them, then you have no more defense. I wish I could persuade you to anyway.

Well, I must shove off...just wanted you to know that the Cowells are opposed to capital punishment...always have been but now it is so much more personal. What a tangled web we weave.

Love,

Edna

P.S. I'll still come if you want to talk—let me know

*The seafood processing ship in Dutch Harbor, Alaska.*

# Unalaska

"We arrived at the end of the earth," I wrote to my parents upon first reaching Dutch Harbor in Unalaska, Alaska on September 9, 1975.

The trip hadn't been an easy one. Eastpoint Seafoods had arranged our travel from Seattle, and after arriving in Anchorage, we'd swapped the commercial airline for Reeve Aleutian, the only operation to get us to our final destination. My first impression of the twin-engine, turbo prop plane had not been positive. My friend Pamela and I, along with the other members of our small group, found seats bolted to the metal deck, separated from piles of supplies by netting, and we anxiously strapped in.

The flight was three and half hours, and I remember it being very loud. As we began to make our descent, it should have come as a relief, but the approach to the landing strip required the pilot to thread through a very narrow valley. I could feel the high winds buffeting the plane outside, and it looked to me that the wings would surely hit the outcroppings of the mountains that rose up, like a beast awakening, on both sides. Powerless in my comfortless, utilitarian seat and with nothing else to do, I squeezed my eyes shut and simply prayed we'd make it.

We did, and I gained deep appreciation for the skill of the Reeve Aleutian pilot. But our arrival was hardly cause for celebration. The first thing we learned upon deplaning was that we had no living quarters. The one-room "cabins" meant to house seasonal workers were still being hastily erected by carpenters. Winds, which we were told could run up to 160 mph and never stopped on those treeless islands, whipped around us as we took in the harbor we'd be calling home for the next few months. Rugged mountains surrounded us, snowcapped despite the early September date. Pamela and I took one look at the rusty ship on which we'd be working, tied to the derelict pier, and we wondered—not for the last time—what we'd gotten ourselves into.

Still, my sense of adventure persisted, carrying me through those first hard weeks, even when we learned that our cabin—a twelve-by-twelve foot windowless shack with a single heater, stacked with bunks where we never had any privacy—wouldn't have a functional bathroom for some time. Almost as soon as we arrived, like an omen, an enormous whale carcass washed ashore on the beach not far from our base, and no matter where we went, we couldn't get away from the stench. But there was a reason my father had always called me his "little free spirit," and I was determined to find the fun in the experience, to appreciate the untamed beauty all the way out there on the far side of nowhere.

Then came the day in early October when I was called to the bridge.

✳ ✳ ✳

Even now, I can still hear John's words in my ear, crackling through the receiver.

"It's Ted."

I don't remember how the conversation finished. I can barely recall hanging up the phone, the plant manager asking me if everything was alright. "Well," I heard my voice as if it belonged to someone else, "well, no." Inside my head, I was already falling into a bottomless hole.

Once I left the bridge, most of what followed is a complete blank, but what I do remember echoes like flashes in my mind.

I remember running through the ship. Just...running.

Racing through my mind, over and over, the thoughts:

*Down is up.*

*White is black.*

*Nothing I thought I knew is true anymore.*

So I ran.

I recalled the feeling of being afraid of monsters under my bed as a little girl. Could it be, the monster hadn't been under my bed at all?

I shook away the thought and kept running, across the deck of the ship overlooking the gloomy harbor, everything salt-rusted, paint chipped, and peeling.

As a ship's horn blasted into the air, drowning out all other sounds, I screamed.

I couldn't stop screaming.

&#42; &#42; &#42;

Eventually, though I don't remember it, I must have returned to my station on the packing line. Pamela watched me float back to the conveyor belt and noted that I seemed quiet. She told me later that she worried I'd received bad news from home, maybe an illness in the family, or a death.

Nothing, though, even close to the truth.

But I couldn't bring myself to tell her right away. I just couldn't talk about it. For the rest of the day, the news sat in my head while regular life went on around me, and I felt the weight of it growing heavier.

Pamela and I had been close for a couple of years, both of us part of a "tribe" of like-minded friends who'd been drawn to Longbranch due, at least in part, to the gravitational pulls of Don, Clarke Palmer, and Far-A-Way. In those years, we'd seen each other through a lot. But still, I didn't know how to tell Pamela something I couldn't even process myself.

It wasn't until that night that I finally conjured up the words, and finding a place where we could speak privately, I told Pamela about John's call.

"I can't believe it," I said to her. "I just can't believe it."

In shock, Pamela agreed with the sentiment. She'd lived in the Puget Sound area much of her life, so she knew all about the murders. And over the years, she'd heard me tell several stories about my cousin Ted, so she understood how close we were, how much I looked up to him.

"It can't be right," she said.

&#42; &#42; &#42;

The more I thought about it, the less sense it made. Instead of coming around to the idea, my mind continued to reject it. But in the terrible fog shone a single light, an idea that acted as a lighthouse beacon. It was the only thing that made sense.

*Maybe it's all a big mistake.*

When they arrested Ted, they must have gotten the wrong guy. That happened sometimes—probably more often than I even realized. And now it had happened to our family.

*The police are wrong*, I thought. *They have to be.*

*Ted is innocent.*

\* \* \*

Despite everything, the work at Dutch Harbor pressed on relentlessly.

The conveyor belt, for which we were responsible, ran twenty-four hours a day in the bowels of the ship. We took shifts, eight of us on the line at a time, or seven on the days when one woman—the fastest packer of all of us—would disappear on benders, and we'd be forced to cover. Machinery whirred and clanked constantly, making it impossible to talk—not that we could have spared the time. We needed to work fast to ensure the crab legs were packed as freshly as possible.

And since this was crabbing season, they just kept coming. Above deck, we'd feel boat after boat unloading their holds, bursting with valuable Alaskan king crab, and the processing ship would groan and tilt under the new weight, the water under our feet sloshing to one side as we adjusted our aching bodies to stay upright. Before they reached us, the crabs were cracked in half, cooked, then run through hydraulics that blew the legs from the shells. Once the cooked crab legs hit the conveyor belt, we hurried to pack them into five-pound cartons, which were then flash-frozen and shipped to Seattle and then all over the world.

We worked agonizingly long shifts on our feet in the damp and cold. Our packing line sat right next to the freezer room, and when they'd open the doors, vapor from the dry ice snaked out and enveloped our legs. We were advised to wear rain gear—not provided by the company—in an attempt to stay dry, but mine was stolen early on, and I had to manage without until I could afford to buy another set.

Our rate was three dollars an hour—four-fifty for overtime—and at the height of the season we were expected to work over thirty days without a day off. When the company asked me if I'd help with their books, I jumped at the chance to get hours off the packing line, but it was to their folly. With access to the books, I had proof when they tried to get away with not paying us, which I shared with the group. It was only when we threatened to strike (Pamela's line: "We won't process your crab until you process our paychecks!") that we received our wages.

The conditions were eye-openingly awful. And yet, through it all, nothing compared to what I was desperately failing to process inside my own head.

\* \* \*

During this time, letters from John and my parents became a lifeline. Though separated by thousands of miles—my parents in Arkansas, John in Seattle, me in Alaska—we all found ourselves in the exact same camp when it came to Ted. None of us could believe the news, and we bolstered one another in our conviction that his arrest had been a mistake. Words like "bizarre" and "poor Ted" littered our letters to one another, and I took unreserved comfort in the knowledge that my loved ones felt the same way I did.

We saw it as our duty to rally behind Ted during his time of unspeakable difficulty. We felt he needed our support more than ever, and I sent him a letter in Utah to try to cheer him up and let him know he could count on us. We remained steadfastly optimistic that the truth would, eventually, prevail. After all, as Ted's family, I felt we could judge matters better than anyone. We knew Ted, and had known him since childhood. Who better to understand than us?

I didn't know, then, that our relation to Ted actually made it impossible for us to see the situation clearly.

\* \* \*

On October 15, 1975, a couple weeks after I'd received the news from John, I was called again to the bridge for a phone call. This time, the voice that greeted me from the other side of the line wasn't one I recognized. The man introduced himself as Detective Robert Keppel of Seattle's homicide department.

As with my call from John, the ship-to-shore technology made our conversation excruciatingly difficult, but I concentrated hard to understand every word Detective Keppel was saying. It was very important to me to help the police. They needed to understand it couldn't have been Ted. They needed to see that the real murderer was still out there.

Detective Keppel wanted to "take my statement," he said, and I readily agreed. He asked me questions about my relationship with Ted and approximately how many times I'd seen him during the first half of 1974. I told him about Ted stopping by my house from time to time and that I thought of him like a brother.

Since he'd already spoken with the other girls I'd lived with in the house off Aurora Avenue and knew a connection existed, he asked me about my relationship to Lynda Ann Healy. I told him I recalled meeting her only one time for certain. He asked if Ted had any connections to Ellensburg, Washington or Corvallis, Oregon, and I recognized the town names from news reports as those from which Susan Elaine Rancourt and Roberta Kathleen Parks had disappeared. To my knowledge, Ted had no links to these locations, but I told Detective Keppel that I might've heard Ted mention an associate from a Republican committee who lived in Oregon.

Working against the difficulties of the phone line, I sought to give my full cooperation. I had nothing to hide or duck, and I wanted the detective to understand this. Unlike him, I knew Ted personally. I could speak to his character. Carefully, so as to make my voice as clear as possible, I tried to explain to the Seattle homicide detective that Ted was a good and moral man, a wonderful cousin, and not someone who could have committed the crimes for which he was suspected.

Detective Keppel listened to everything I had to say, taking notes. Before ending the call, he asked me if I'd ever noticed any "weird behavior" from Ted, even as a child. "Does anything come to mind?" he asked. "Anything at all?"

"No," I told him, and it was the truth.

# Letter from Edna to Her Parents

*Sent From Dutch Harbor, Alaska.*

*Transcription of entire letter.*

September 10th, 1975

Dear Mother & Father,

We arrived at the end of the earth yesterday at 5:00, 7:00 Seattle time. When we arrived at camp the women's quarters were half done. Our bungalow which sleeps six had no windows, no electricity and no bathroom. They brought in mattresses around seven o'clock and by nine the windows were put in place, the lights were working and we were issued one heater. Our bathroom should be finished by the end of the week, hopefully.

We haven't started working yet which is actually one of our saving graces. We had to scrounge for bedding last night and some of us got a little chilly.

The weather is damp but not too cold. There are no trees but the islands are mountainous and covered with alpine meadows. It is quite stunning. The harbor is surrounded by hills coming straight up from the shores. There is a little town [Unalaska] across the bay that looks quite picturesque. The church is definitely Russian influenced in its architecture... onion domes.

There are quite a few [native people (Aleuts)] inhabiting the Aleutians. There is a fairly large school over in [Unalaska] where children from all over come by water. A bottle of whiskey sells for $13.50. Thank God I'm not an alcoholic.

I took some pictures this morning. Whether they turn out is debatable. It's quite cloudy. Mist is swirling up over the mountain peaks and there are patches of snow on surrounding peaks of higher elevation than we [are].

There has been a lot of talk of extremely high winds...up to 120-160 mph. I am having a hard time coming to grips with that aspect of nature's role here. I may just blow away...maybe I can hitch a ride on a zephyr to Tahiti.

The food is plentiful and quite tasty. We had turkey and mashed potatoes last night. We eat on the ship East Point. We will be spending a lot of time on her in the months to come.

They showed a movie last night, *Billy Jack*, but Pam and I were too tired to watch it. We had been on various planes for 9 hours yesterday and we were beginning to feel rather rung out. We flew Alaska Airlines to Juneau, [Anchorage]. Then we changed to Reeve Aleutian Airlines and got on a plane that looked like something out of World War II. I was quite apprehensive but the flight went smoothly and we all arrived safely.

September 15th

Today we did our first full day of work. I worked 5 hours yesterday doing office work but that in no way compared to the work today.

We started work at 8:00 and worked until 6:00. About 8 of us worked on a conveyor belt packing the meat of crab legs into long rectangular boxes. Can you imagine doing that for 10 hours? I ate some of the crab and it is the best crab I have ever eaten. Alaska King Crab is exquisite, especially when it is fresh.

There were several exciting occurrences today. There was an electrical fire which scared the daylights out of us. When you are standing in several inches of water and sparks and flames come shooting down from the ceiling you tend to want to get the heck out. But, everything was under control in a matter of minutes. A couple of hours later, oil started dripping from the ceiling and was culminated by an exploding oil line. There was oil everywhere. When the oil line broke, the machinery ground to a halt for lack of lubrication. After they repaired the machinery 1 ½ hours later, the conveyor belts started up again. But, the noise level is absolutely punitive. It is horrible. They should do something about it.

Anyway, here I am working my little body like crazy. It is hard to imagine doing it for 3 months because it is monotonous.

There's a movie showing tonight with Jane Fonda and Brigitte Bardot. I think I'll pass. I worked an extra 2 hours tonight—got a little over-time.

Well, I must send this to you so that you will write to me. It is exciting to get mail—I haven't received any yet.

I feel like this is quite an adventure.

Love you all a whole lot.

Edna

# Letter from John to Edna in Dutch Harbor

*(Note what revelation occurs midway through John's writing.)*

*Transcription of entire letter.*

October 4, 1975

Dear Edna,

I am glad to hear from you. Mother read me your letter. When I worked at Campbell Soup, the assembly line was always breaking down.

I'm really interested in the weather there. Unalaska looks like the northern Scottish islands. I hope you can find fun things to do even with the long shifts.

I spent Sept. 21-22 lying on a beach (North of Taylor Bay, South of Vaughn). The temperature got near 90. I swam a lot. Yesterday, Oct 1, it was 83 degrees. The leaves haven't begun to turn yet. Last night I had a surprise visit by my friend Cathy with 6 lamb chops. We made salads and burned candles and talked about ourselves. She read my poetry. I looked at her paintings—what a treat.

I hear rain outside. I'm glad to hear it wash the smog away.

Right now, I am working on putting together a Consultantship—wish me luck.

* * *

Oh my God! Cousin Louise just called me. Ted is being held in Utah for the murder-disappearances of a number of women out there. They are also trying to pin the murder of 8 women in King County on him. I will send you more info. I am really feeling sorry for Ted. This is really bizarre and terrible.

I am thinking of you with love and support.

Love

John

Oh my God! Cousin Louise just called
me. Ted is being held in Utah
for the murder disappearances of a
number of women out there. They are also trying to
pin the murder of 8 women in King County on
him. I will send you more info.
I am really feeling sorry for Ted
This is really bizarre and terrible

I am thinking of you with love and
support.

Love John

# Letter from Parents to Edna in Dutch Harbor

*Transcription of letter excerpt.*

October 8, 1975

Dearest Edna,

[My mother wrote] I called Ginny—she's gasping about poor Ted. I sent him a book of stamps—When I called Louise back to tell her again of our support she said she loved me—so you know she's grateful for a nice word or two—she had two policemen there while I was talking, asking her questions. I told her about your left-handed attacker and told her to ask if that was a piece of evidence. What was the color of his hair? Ted's height?

[My dad wrote] Try to stay very positive and not brood over Ted. Everything will be done.

Love Dad and Love Mother

# Letter from John to Edna in Dutch Harbor

*Transcription of letter excerpt.*

October 27, 1975

Dear Edna,

I read a letter to Richard Larson of the *Seattle Times* from Ted. It said that the huge outpouring of support for him has been heartening and that he is doing fine. He goes on that the legal process is impersonal to the law student but now that he is a defendant, the process looks humane in its fairness—the rights afforded the accused are not found anywhere in the world. "I am confident that the end result will be a good product."

Edna, I will be preparing some news articles for you about Ted. There is otherwise a total news blackout on the subject from the lawyers/DAs involved.

I think I will go up to talk to [Don's friend Michael from the prosecutor's office] soon. The whole family is mobilizing around Ted now so I am confident he will be cared for.

I talked to King County Homicide for 3 hours. They said they have nothing on Ted. Ted's lawyer says that the accusation of evading an officer is a bunch of garbage.

# Letter from Parents to Edna in Dutch Harbor

*Transcription of letter excerpt.*

November 3, 1975

[From my mother] We got a very cheerful letter from Ted today—your father has to Xerox it so we can send you a copy—He had gotten your letter and loved it. He's had his bail reduced to $15,000! Isn't that a wonderful happening! It shows they don't consider him a mad killer any more. Louise is going to take a loan on their cabin to raise the $1500— that's all you have to give the bondsman so he'll pay for you—10% that is—so that's cheerful news. Your Uncle David sent Louise $500 after Jack called and asked him for a donation. Isn't that amazing? I think he should call Larry now. I'm only sending $25 this month. Alas—maybe more after I use my adding machine.

[From my dad] We talked to John a long time about Ted's bail being reduced 10 times (to a 10th, $150,000 to $15,000) and he was sure it meant they didn't have a real case!

This is all so bizarre!

## Letter from Ted to Edna's Parents

*Written from prison in Utah, after Edna sent Ted a letter of support.*
*Copy of letter was included with letter from parents.*

*Transcription of entire letter.*

Tuesday, October 28, 1975

Dear Eleanor and Jack:

I am less preoccupied about the nuances of prison life than I was initially. I know the ground rules and they are the ground rules which apply to my group of people confined under stress. Perhaps the day will come when I can collect my impressions more rationally than now. I do my own thing: absorb myself in a book; lose myself in writing. Mental calisthenics. The mind is strong. The fighting spirit lives.

Edna wrote a lovely letter to me from the frontier. The fish are running; the snow is falling; the natives are restless; and the ghost of Jack London lives in your daughter. I am sure her life up there must terrify you at times. I find it fascinating. Somewhat romantic. I envy Edna, hard work and all.

Today was one of those confidence building days. Received ten letters. Talked with my attorney. And became appointed to convey the inmates' grievances about the diet, an appointment I accepted with hesitation. I've always been a sucker for a free meal and it has never occurred to me to complain about three free per day. If these guys were on the outside, they'd complain about the weather. Since jails have no weather, the quality of the food is a vulnerable issue. Assuming my role as honorary attorney, I grieved (I think that's the word he chose) in good faith.

Mother says you have called her several times. Bless you. Last time I telephoned she sounded so good. I know your support strengthens her.

Love to you both,

ted

*Young Ted (right) with John (left) and Sam Cowell (center) holding Baby.*

# The Ted Bundy

When I left Alaska, I couldn't have weighed more than a hundred pounds.

I blamed my weight loss on supply shortages on the island. I couldn't remember the last time I'd eaten fresh fruit, vegetables, milk, or meat. It seemed any real nutritional staples had disappeared from the galley. And, in the middle of nowhere, we didn't exactly have other resources.

However, Pamela told me later that hadn't been her experience at all. She, in fact, remembered the opposite. Additionally, since we had the greenlight to eat as much of the crab as we wanted—picking whole legs straight off the belt as they were delivered steaming from the cookers—and with few other indulgences, she found it harder not to gain weight during her time at Dutch Harbor.

I was forced to face the truth. Something deeper had caused my dramatic physical change.

After the day I received John's phone call on the bridge, I threw myself into work, searching for not comfort exactly—more like immersion—in the back-breaking, mind-numbing labor. A kind of parasitic symbiosis occurred. The job asked for everything, and at that time, everything was exactly what I was prepared to give. After all, only when my body was aching and spent did I reach an exhaustion so thick that no unwanted thoughts could infiltrate.

I was in Dutch Harbor for two and a half months, but it felt more like two and a half lifetimes. By November, as the Alaskan king crab season was wrapping up and we were nearing the end of our contract at Eastpoint Seafoods, the days had gotten shorter with the sun setting around 4:30 p.m. Storms rolled through with more frequency, and the ever-constant wind—unimpeded by the treeless Aleutian landscape—caused loose rigging on the ships and fishing boats to clang incessantly. Crossing the harbor in skiffs grew more and more unpleasant, as the boats navigated the choppy water, and the spray drenched all on board. Despite all I'd be returning to, I was ready to go home.

Those who lasted the entire season had their airfare back to Seattle paid for. Out of the original crew of about a hundred processors, only twelve remained. Pamela and I were two of the twelve.

The morning of November 30, 1975, Pam and I again climbed aboard the Reeve Aleutian Airlines twin turbo-prop plane, buckled in, and leaned back for the 1,200-mile flight back to Anchorage. From there, we caught an Alaska Airlines flight to Seattle, another 1,500 miles.

This gave me a lot of time with nothing to do but reflect on what I was coming home to. Thoughts I'd worked to keep out of my head seeped in like dark water.

Ted.

Immediately, I recalled the allegations from John's call. Kidnapper. Rapist. Serial murderer. The words alone conjured an image in my mind of a monster, a devil, a perverted beast straight out of a fevered nightmare. No one in their right mind could commit those acts. I wasn't exactly religious, but it occurred to me that this type of appetite must be the manifestation of Satan himself. I hoped the detective had believed me—that was not Ted. That couldn't be farther from Ted.

Sick from such visions, I tucked them aside again, finding it easier to turn my thoughts to Don. Unfortunately, such thoughts did little to soothe my nerves. Our time apart had given me much to consider. In the beginning, Don had written one or two letters, but after that...nothing. Being as isolated as we were, we depended on contact from home. Didn't he realize that? Sure, I received steady correspondence from my parents and other friends, but that only made his silence more pronounced. The more I thought about it, the more I read into his blackout. Had he lost interest? Was he seeing someone else? In the throes of that other—much darker—emotional turbulence, I admit I may have compounded outrage in Don's direction. Not that he didn't deserve it.

By the time I finally made it to Seattle, I'd gotten myself pretty worked up. I made a plan. Don was staying with our friend, Clarke, at Far-A-Way while Clarke's parents wintered in Southern California. I'd go there and confront him. I had to know if he was in or out.

I hopped into my Ford Country Squire wagon and made the ninety-minute drive to Longbranch. Pulling up to Far-A-Way, I parked at the end of the pergola next to the '65 blue Bonneville convertible I knew well: Don's car. That meant the bastard was home.

I headed down the two-hundred-foot walkway, getting angrier with every step. By the time I slammed open the door to the kitchen, I was ready to read Don the riot act.

Inside, Margie was sitting in the kitchen with her boyfriend. Their shock as the door burst open rendered them speechless, and they could only watch, slack-jawed, as I stormed past. I barely even registered their presence, laser-focused on finding Don.

Rounding into the living room, my eyes landed on a woman around my age. I knew that Clarke had a new girlfriend named Ann, and for the sake of this speechless figure staring in shock, I hoped to God that was the name on her driver's license.

I strode right past her and beelined to Don, who looked almost as stunned as she did.

"Why didn't you write to me?!" I didn't beat around the bush. "I was stuck in that godforsaken place without a word from you. Didn't you care?"

Don, who on a normal day could hold a conversation with a brick wall, was at a loss for words.

Margie and her boyfriend had inched towards the living room to see what was going on, and right about then, Clarke walked in, just to give our little drama an even bigger audience. He stopped dead in his tracks. Clarke had known me since I was about six years old, and he told me later he'd never seen me like this before (or since, for that matter).

Noticing our captive audience, Don suggested the two of us go for a walk. Gently, he took my arm and led me out to the porch and down the steps. As we walked, I quieted enough to allow him to explain himself. He said he's always been a terrible writer, finding it difficult to put his thoughts down on paper. When I lived in Arkansas, he reminded me, he got his friend Mike—a gifted letter writer, I can attest—to write for him. That didn't mean he wasn't thinking about me—because he was. All the time.

What can I say? I was assuaged. I challenge anyone who's seen a photo of Don from this time period to hold me blame. After being apart for months, I took a good look at this man and knew I didn't want to be apart again. He must have felt the same way.

We were married six months later.

Annie, who was indeed the figure in the living room, has now been my friend for over fifty years despite my dramatic first impression. It does make a good story to tell when our families get together.

* * *

With that issue solved, it was time to face the other.

Concerned about how skinny I was, Don's favorite pastime became taking me to restaurants, ordering multiple dishes, then watching, in disturbed fascination, as I ate them all myself. My appetite was bottomless. Proudly, he'd signal to the server—*keep 'em coming*—as he slid his own untouched plate in front of me.

On these occasions, we talked a lot about Ted.

Like me, my brother had called Don to deliver the news, only Don hadn't been available. Having received word that John was trying to reach him, Don dropped by an auto parts distributor on South Tacoma Way where his friend Doug worked, and from there he returned John's call.

As John broke the news of Ted's arrest in Salt Lake City, Don was so utterly stunned by John's words, he kept repeating them aloud to Doug, trying to process them himself. Hearing what Don was doing on the other end of the line, John got angry and told Don to stop repeating family business. I can think of no better instance to demonstrate how we all had our own ways to try to get a handle on the news. Don needed support and feedback. John needed to contain the fallout.

Like me, and like everyone else at that time who knew Ted personally, Don didn't believe it.

This is the messy reality, the unvarnished truth. People ask me what it's like to be related to a man like Ted, and this is a big piece of it: we're the hardest to convince.

But it's not only blood relations. Everyone who thought of Ted as a friend—and he had many—could not wrap their minds around the news. Any doubts were explained away. To accept that Ted could be capable of the actions of which he was being accused, even as a possibility, would be to open ourselves to a pain unlike anything else, and the body is evolved to avoid pain.

To be a family member or good friend of a man like Ted means your body is physiologically disposed to reject the truth.

Sitting in all those diners and cafes, Don and I agreed the allegations against Ted had to be, as he said, "a total smoke job." Ted was a former Boy Scout, a law student, an up-and-coming Young Republican who was always polite to strangers and used to volunteer at a crisis center. "Young Republicans don't kidnap and murder people," Don said, and I agreed. We weren't being naive, we assured ourselves. He just wasn't the type who could do something like this. We knew the real Ted.

I know now we both had little voices buried deep in our unconscious minds, trying to get our attention, but we desperately didn't want them to be correct, so we silenced them.

For Don's part, it was a nagging worry over some things he'd been hearing recently in the news. First of all, that damn duffel bag Utah police had found in Ted's car contained, among other suspicious items, a crowbar and a mask made from pantyhose. Holes had been cut out, two eyes and a mouth. What possible innocent explanation was there for that? *Maybe he's a peeping tom*, Don thought. *But definitely not a killer.* John believed that Ted might've taken up burglarizing, which would also account for the expensive ski equipment he'd seen in Ted's apartment. Either explanation Don was more prepared to wrap his mind around.

But even more troubling to him was the key. It had been found in the parking lot where Debra Kent had disappeared, and it matched the handcuffs found on Carol DaRonch after she'd escaped being abducted—the same woman who had identified Ted from a police lineup as her would-be kidnapper. That key was harder to rationalize. Even though he brushed the thought aside, it needled Don's subconscious, suggesting that the attempted kidnapping charge, already worse than window-peeping and burglary, was possibly only the tip of an even uglier iceberg.

For my part, the niggling voice was buried deeper—Ted was family after all—and born more of self-protection, a doomsday-like paranoia to be prepared for the unimaginable. Simply put, I knew the accusations about Ted couldn't be true! (But what if they were?) Ted was a great guy! (But what if he wasn't?)

There was only one way for me to get that voice out of my head once and for all, which I needed to do or I'd go crazy. Quite satisfied by how well things had panned out with Don, it seemed only sensible to stick with the same strategy.

I had to confront Ted.

❊ ❊ ❊

As luck would have it, Ted was released on bail in December when the Salt Lake City judge agreed to reduce the amount from $150,000 to $15,000, a decision that strengthened our belief that the state didn't have a case against him. With the bail paid, Ted was not only out of jail but coming back to Seattle.

As I began to look into where he'd be living and how to get a hold of him, my efforts became unnecessary.

Ted called me himself.

He'd just gotten into town, he said, and he wanted to see me. He hoped to hear about Alaska and catch up. This was my opportunity. Anxious to talk, I told him I'd be meeting some Dutch Harbor friends for lunch at the Deluxe 2 Restaurant near University Village, and I suggested he come along. Ted eagerly agreed.

But, he said, he'd need a ride.

He didn't mention the reason—that he'd sold his beloved Volkswagen after authorities started closing in on him—that, even still, police had managed to hunt it down, and the FBI in Utah had had it impounded and dismantled for evidence.

That nagging in my head buzzed, but I swatted it away. Cheerfully, I made arrangements to pick him up.

❊ ❊ ❊

Ted was staying with his girlfriend, Liz, at the time, and I pulled up to her house in my Squire wagon. As Ted emerged, all smiles, and made his way down the porch steps, I couldn't help but note how normal this all seemed. I was going to lunch with my cousin. Versions of this exact scenario had played out so many times, they weren't worth recounting.

When he piled inside, he reached across the long bench seat and pulled me into a hug. He felt the way he always did. Smelled the way he always did. I had told myself to go into this encounter with an open mind, but I found my resolve slipping. With Ted sitting beside me, I felt more sure than ever that the police had made a mistake.

That's all there was to it.

\* \* \*

My friends were seated at a round table when we arrived. On seeing each other, we hugged in a welcome befitting the solidarity of soldiers back from war. I was gratified to see the same warmth extended to my cousin. Grabbing an extra chair from a nearby table, Ted wedged in close a little behind me, and I leaned forward to make sure he was part of the group.

Discussion of our shared time in "Dutch," the nickname we all called the harbor, carried us through most of the meal. But as plates cleared and forks began to be set down, one of the guys across the table, likely only to be polite, turned his attention to Ted.

"Ted, right?" he said. "Ted what?"

My stomach dropped. For the first time since returning, my appetite vanished, and I urged the food I'd just consumed to stay where it was.

"Bundy," Ted said.

The guy's voice went up an octave. "Not *the* Ted Bundy."

All side conversations at the table ceased. I could only watch, helpless. What had I been thinking, bringing Ted along, placing him in this position? Of course his name was in the papers. Of course he was of acute interest to the public. But, unlike me, they didn't understand that he couldn't be guilty. I was still leaning forward then and couldn't bear to look back at him, feeling as awful as I did, so I didn't see Ted's expression when he replied,

"Yep. *The* Ted Bundy."

Stunned, the motion of turning back to face him felt more like falling off a cliff. Was that...pride in his voice?

Before I could get my bearings, the mood at the table turned. Here we sat just outside the University District, the very neighborhood that had become the hunting ground of a vicious predator. Memory of fear was still thick in the air, perhaps not even yet relegated to memory—reluctance to go out after dark still shaped plans, self-defense classes continued to fill to capacity, windows remained locked tight in any weather. These past two years had fundamentally changed the community—even the world—and now my group of friends found themselves at a table with the man thought to be responsible. Eyes grew into saucers. The girl pressed in on Ted's right actually recoiled away. The tension was palpable, but somehow Ted didn't sense it. Or worse...

He did, and he took pleasure in it.

As I watched, Ted sat up straighter, puffing out his chest.

I felt so disoriented, I had to check to make sure I was still sitting and that my chair was still rooted to the floor. The room seemed to tilt. It was almost as if I was back in the bowels of the processing ship in Alaska, and a heavy delivery upstairs had caused my whole world to list.

Meanwhile, the guy across the table, the one who'd innocently cracked open this can of worms, had an altogether different reaction from the others. It was a reaction I would become more and more familiar with in coming years. He ogled Ted as if meeting a celebrity.

And Ted soaked it up.

It was as if the attention actually made Ted expand and grow larger.

It was all too much. Wedged in by Ted's chair, I suddenly felt trapped, and I couldn't stand it. Abruptly I stood, forcing Ted to scoot back, and slapped money on the table for our food. Frazzled, I made hasty good-byes, telling the group that I had an errand to run. Then with Ted on my heels, I rushed outside.

* * *

Catching up to me on the sidewalk, Ted asked if I was alright, so I assured him I was fine. I just had to run to (here I looked around wildly, trying to remember where in the world we were) the University Bookstore for a few things. I'd only be a minute.

Back in the Squire as I accelerated up the hill towards the U-District, there was silence in the cab. This was it, I knew. No use avoiding it any longer. It was time to ask the question.

"So, Ted." I stared ahead out the windshield. Why was this so hard? I tried to take comfort from the cheery pedestrians outside, the store-fronts decorated for the holidays, life carrying on as usual. I screwed up my courage. "Did you do it?"

That buried voice in my subconscious now screamed. What I was actually asking, but was far too afraid to say, was, "Did you kidnap, rape, and murder all those girls like they're saying?"

He didn't respond at first, and in that silence, a part of me died. It struck me then, for the first time, that he could answer yes, and if he did, I had no idea what I'd do. I took my eyes off the road to look at him.

He smiled, a very familiar Cowell smile, and shrugged.

"Edna," he said, "of course not." Completely relaxed, he went on to explain that it was all a case of mistaken identity, and that the truth would come out eventually. He said exactly what I'd suspected and hoped.

Unaware that I'd stopped breathing, I let out a breath so deep I could feel it in my toes. As he continued to reassure me, even teasing me for needing to ask, I experienced a kind of euphoria. I felt light, filled with helium.

What had I been worried about? This was my cousin. The guy who'd gone out of his way to visit us in Arkansas and told me my new drawl was cute. The guy who'd regularly shown up on my doorstep in the U-District with a bag of groceries, offering to cook dinner.

I looked over at Ted and beamed. Call it confirmation bias, call it familial immunity, but I believed him. Everything would be fine, I knew then. Just fine. I couldn't wait to tell Don we were right.

✳ ✳ ✳

Feeling much better, I parked the Squire in the lot behind the University Bookstore and told Ted I'd only be a minute. As I shut the door behind me, I felt safer—though I wouldn't acknowledge why—knowing Ted was securely tucked away in the shaded back parking lot.

Inside the bookstore, I quickly gathered my purchases and brought them to the line of registers, which fronted floor-to-ceiling windows facing the street. A clerk greeted me and began to ring me up.

I dully registered some commotion outside. As I dug inside my purse for my wallet, in my peripheral view, a small group of co-eds ran southward past the large windows.

It wasn't until I'd finished paying that the events outside finally penetrated my consciousness. By then, it seemed all pedestrian traffic was flowing in the direction of 43rd Street, attracted to some magnetic pole. Many people were pointing and angling for view.

Just like that, my head began to throb. I was suddenly in a hurry to leave, and I barely remembered to grab my purchases on my way out.

As I stepped onto the sidewalk, I was immediately engulfed into a throng proceeding down University Way.

"What's going on?" I asked those around me, but no one seemed to know. I craned my neck to see the other side of the street where the crowds were congealing, but I couldn't make out the cause.

Reaching the end of the block, I had to wait for the light to change to cross. For a brief moment, the sea of bodies on the other side parted such that I caught one small glimpse into the crowd's nucleus, and I recognized Ted.

*What's he doing there?* I looked anxiously at the light, still holding me where I was. I had to get to him. I didn't know why, but I knew I had to stop him.

Finally the light changed, and the crowd advanced, flowing around Ted like water. Many stopped to stare in fascinated horror, forming a kind of standing-room-only arena surrounding him. Somehow I pushed through them, and there I got my first good look.

This is the image that probably haunts me most, the image that still, fifty years later, makes my heart rate surge.

Ted's arms were outstretched wide, a street-corner messiah, and he was slowly turning in a circle. From his smiling lips, he chanted over and over, projecting for all to hear,

"I'm Ted Bundy. I'm Ted Bundy. I'm Ted Bundy."

My first thought was that he, in fact, wasn't Ted, because I suddenly didn't recognize him in the slightest. Then instantly my mind raced back to the moment when I'd experienced the same disorientation—the night Ted slow-danced with Margie in our apartment after dinner.

As he turned on the street corner, I could again picture him turning with Margie in his arms. In both cases, the Ted I knew had completely disappeared. I knew then with certainty, as I watched him speak those horrible words, that Ted had another side, a darker side, and it was that Ted whom I was seeing.

If, up to that point, I'd been viewing the world through rose-colored glasses, this was the moment they shattered.

As my mind reeled, all around me the crowds became a blur, but I was distantly aware they were turning hostile. It was clear that I had to do something. I felt completely outside myself as I ran into the swarm.

"*Stop it! Shut up!*"

But he didn't stop.

Desperate—and Don couldn't believe me when I told him this later—I slapped a hand over Ted's mouth. Who was I, behaving like this in public? I didn't recognize myself at all. All I knew was that I didn't want the crowds to witness Ted doing whatever it was he was doing. *I* didn't want to witness him doing it any longer. Even then, in the chaos of the moment, I knew it had dislodged something important inside me.

Finally Ted yielded, and the masses parted as I dragged him away, guiding him toward the back lot where I'd parked the car. I knew we had an audience, but I couldn't think about that then. I wanted nothing more than to get away.

"What the hell were you doing?" I really needed to get a handle on my emotions, but adrenaline still coursed through my veins as I turned on the engine and sped into the street.

Watching the mob shrink in the rearview mirror, I was finally able to take a breath. But the reprieve, I found, was far worse. In the silence of the car, I realized that buried voice had been knocked right to the surface, and it was now impossible to ignore as it laid out its case.

Fact 1: I'd witnessed a completely different side of Ted that day, at lunch but especially outside the bookstore. This was a Ted I didn't recognize or understand. This was a Ted who frightened me.

Fact 2: He operated in a way totally alien to my fundamental moral compass. Women had been brutally raped and murdered, their bodies defiled, yet he seemed to suffer no horror at his association, whether true or not. Indeed, his actions showed that he felt *proud*.

Fact 3, and this was the one I really didn't want to face; the one I knew then, without a shade of doubt:

Ted was guilty.

My cousin, who was more like a brother. My teaser and protector and confidant. My friend.

He'd done it. All of it.

The images I'd conjured of a nightmare beast resurfaced, and a chill passed down my spine as another truth reared its head.

I was alone with a cold-blooded killer.

Me, still barely a hundred pounds.

Inch by inch, I turned my head to look at Ted. On my life, I swear it seemed that I was looking as if through the wrong end of a telescope— an invisible lens stretching the distance of the Ford's bench seat—so that Ted appeared a great distance away. Nothing separated us but vinyl and air.

Ted was staring at me.

Ted was smiling. But this smile held no family resemblance at all.

No words were spoken, but I knew. Ted knew.

My fear represented a power he had over me, and I could sense he liked it.

Suddenly the Squire couldn't go fast enough. As I drove on, rigid with terror, I kept replaying a scenario in my head: if he moved toward me, I'd wrench the wheel and ram my precious car straight into a wall. I'd do it, if I had to. I was ready. I was ready.

I still think about that.

\* \* \*

When I dropped him off, there was no pretense of "see you soon," or "let's plan something next week." Ted swung his legs out of the Squire and walked up the lawn, where I watched him disappear inside the house.

*Ted in various family Christmas photos.
The handwritten note is from Louise.*

# Ripples

*This isn't good; this isn't good; this isn't good.*

The words repeated in my head, over and over, as I raced home.

I glanced across the bench seat to the passenger's side, now empty. The more I replayed what had just happened, the more I began to believe that the man sitting next to me hadn't been Ted at all, but some monster I didn't know he harbored inside him.

What other women had found themselves alone in a car with him, and what had happened next? Had he smiled at them the way he'd smiled at me?

It was too horrible to think about. But in the echo chamber of the car, speeding down familiar streets I never even registered, I couldn't stop.

\* \* \*

Don was furious.

Not at me, at Ted.

When I finally arrived home and burst into the house, I was barely able to catch my breath. "Oh, my God," I said to an unsuspecting Don. "Oh, my God." Then the words, for the first time, spilled out of my mouth:

"He did it."

Don's initial instinct was to try to calm me down by defending Ted, but I held up my hand to stop him. Then I recounted everything that had just occurred.

To his immense credit, Don believed me, fully and immediately. And he was appalled.

Despite the clear evidence that I was already home safe, he couldn't get over the worry of what *might have* happened. The position I had put myself in by being alone with a man suspected of murder.

To this, I had no excuse. Internally I was berating myself on the same point. *How could I have confronted Ted while I was alone with him?* Over the course of one afternoon, my worldview had shifted so dramatically, I already couldn't understand why I'd ever thought that was a good idea.

It brought back a similar feeling of disorientation to the one I'd felt years earlier in the Arkansas hospital after my mother's brain aneurysm. That day had aged me more than I thought possible in such a short time. But somehow this change was even more dramatic.

I was a completely different person.

* * *

I don't want to give the impression that the transformation resulting from the truth about Ted was instantaneous, however. How does a mind process something like this, reassigning an adored cousin to one of the most well-known serial killers of the twentieth century?

It's an agonizing evolution. The ripples hit me in stages, each one resisted, each one painful.

* * *

One of the first things I remember feeling was a heavy sorrow for the Bundy family. For all my suffering, what in the world could this be like for them? Ted was their golden boy. His mother especially was so proud of his accomplishments. His brothers and sisters depended on him, worshiped him, wanted to be like him.

My heart broke into pieces for the Bundys, and those particular pieces will never fit back together.

* * *

A question hit me like a punch in the stomach. *How did I not know?* Ted and I were close. I loved him, trusted him like a brother.

I began a practice I'd continue, rigorously, for the rest of my life. I began searching through my memories for indicators. Signposts I'd missed along the way.

It's the same question, politely softened, that others inevitably ask when they learn who I am, who I'm related to. *Looking back, were there signs?*

They want to know about the childhood pets he tortured. The neighborhood children who mysteriously went missing. They want to know about the abuse Ted suffered himself.

But to their dismay, I can't speak towards anything like that because the truth is I never saw those things nor had any reason to believe they happened. I can't positively say they didn't, but I can only speak from my experience. My memories.

So these are the ones I come back to:

Jeffy's barking, his bites at Ted's pant legs, impossible to calm.

Ted stoned and wild, dancing on the coffee table.

His hunting glances around the Windjammer's sweaty floor.

The darkness in his face as he slow-danced with Margie.

These are the memories my mind buzzes around, touched up and reinforced over the years.

*Were there signs?*

It's a losing question. The answer I greatly prefer is *yes*, but I didn't see them at the time. The signs were there, but I foolishly missed them all. I was blind. Stupid. Naive.

This is the answer I like.

Because the other answer is, I suspect, the one people are begging me to refute when they ask me the question. It's the possibility no one wants, including myself.

No. There were no signs. Nothing out of the ordinary.

If that's true, it means Ted could be anyone. Even those we'd never suspect. That means it's possible to have everyone fooled.

No one wants that.

✳ ✳ ✳

What would I have done without Don?

As my world fell apart, he stood by my side, which is precisely where he's stayed. After all, it was his world, too.

Not for the last time, I realized how grateful I was that he was in my life—that he was *already* in my life. Because of Ted, everything I thought I knew about people was violently thrown into question. But Don was already on the inside.

Could I have let him in anyway, if I'd met him after? I like to think so. But I'm grateful that I never had to find out.

Because along with a few other life-long friends—Margie, Pamela, Annie—Don's a crucial piece of the construction of my life. He's a load-bearing wall. The solidness of him beside me, stubbornly moral, provided the counterpoint to Ted. As I put all of humanity on trial, Don silently acted as its defense.

He's proof that people can be good.

\* \* \*

When I think of Ted on the street corner that day, the memory still makes me break into a sweat. And yet I understand that glimpse at his other side was also a gift. It set me hurtling on a new trajectory, and only from that vantage point could I begin to see the truth.

But I sensed that my perspective was rapidly changing from that of others who knew Ted, especially those in the family, who hadn't seen what I'd seen. This dissonance, in itself, brought confusion and pain.

My parents were on the other side of the country, and their main source of news on the topic was Louise, who stood by Ted until the bitter end. My father always had a soft spot for Louise. Their bond was what had compelled him to invite her and Ted to Tacoma to live with my family in the first place. I like to think my relationship to Ted had echoed my father's relationship to Louise—of course until it hadn't.

But that bond acted as a blinder for my parents to see the truth.

Though we always remained close and communicated regularly, honestly it got to the point where my parents and I stopped talking about Ted. We'd said everything we had to say, and the topic only brought pain, so when Ted was first found guilty of kidnapping and assault in Salt Lake City, I had no idea that my father, at the urging of Louise, wrote a letter to Judge Stewart Hanson Jr. on Ted's behalf. It wasn't until years later when I found a copy of the letter that I discovered the truth.

In the letter, my father makes a case for a lighter sentence based on Ted's potential and his belief that Ted could still emerge from prison to benefit society. But it all builds toward one particular point which, I believe, reveals where my father was on his own journey at that time.

"Might there be lurking doubts," my father wrote, referring to the guilty verdict, "which would even more strongly suggest leniency?" This was a man who still desperately wanted to believe in Ted's innocence.

It's a difficult letter to read now, in hindsight's stark light. But in it I see how powerfully my father cared for his family.

And, of course, how thoroughly Ted had deceived us.

\* \* \*

I wouldn't say it's hard for me to trust now; I'd say I've gotten better at it.

After Ted, I was blasted into a parallel universe. Everything looked the same but was fundamentally off. My comfortable normal was gone.

Now I assume every person has a side they're not showing, secrets they're holding close. It's a new angle to view the world—not good or bad, just different.

I hold to a motto: *Trust, but don't be deceived.*

Step forward, but keep one foot ready to bolt.

If you were to meet me, you'd probably see me as open, ready to welcome you into my life. And I am, or I try to be.

But my mind is always on your other side—the one you're not showing.

So I smile.

But I watch.

And I wait.

## Letter from John R. Cowell
## to Judge Stewart Hanson Jr.

*Regarding the sentencing of Theodore Bundy in Salt Lake City.*

*Transcription of entire letter.*

Fayetteville, Arkansas

March 14, 1976

Judge Stewart Hanson Jr.

Salt Lake County Courthouse

Salt Lake City, Utah 84111

Dear Judge Hanson:

I feel most urgently compelled to add my voice to those many I am sure are making heartfelt petitions at this time in [sic] behalf of leniency in the sentencing of Theodore Bundy.

I wish to stress my long knowledge of Ted (since early childhood) in offering my conviction that he is a most uncommonly gifted, attractive and sensitive person who still should be considered to represent a potentially valuable human resource. Is it not the end desire of corrections systems to develop useful, helpful prisoners with the eventual purpose of rehabilitation into a beneficial return to society? To this end I make this anguished petition:

First, please, in choice of place of confinement, do not expose him to incarceration with those considered criminally vile and irredeemable; and

Second, consider the many good reports on his character and achievements in selecting a lighter sentence.

Ted and his mother lived with me and my wife and son for nearly a year at our home in Tacoma, Washington when I was a young fledgling faculty member (in the School of Music) at the University of Puget Sound. Both our son and Ted were only four years of age at the time but Ted has always remained like a close and loving member of our family and like a brother to our son and our daughter who was born the year following. Ted's mother is the daughter of my oldest brother. His family, our whole family, the Bundy family subsequently have all lived lives that have been more than exemplary. Such a dark shadow of trouble with the law is the first and only ever, and is a subject of shock, desperate dismay, and incredulity on the parts of all of us.

Since 1959 I have traveled extensively as a concert pianist and composer and since 1966 I have been on the faculty of the University of Arkansas where I came to head the Department of Music. Hence, we have kept in touch with Ted only through annual visits, letters, and second hand accounts from our two children who returned to the Seattle area several years ago. But everything we have seen of or heard of Ted has given us every reason to be proud of not only his progress but even more of his articulate self-expression, his sophisticated manners and knowledge of the world through which he gave us always a sincere and reassuring impression of high aspirations coupled with a strong sense of social and ethic [sic] responsibility. All of the Cowell family on both coasts and in between regard the revelations of press accounts as what can only be called shocking incongruity. Might there not be lurking doubts, therefore, which would even more strongly suggest leniency?

A great weight of the future of a most unusual young man lies in your hands and in the hands of the Probation and Parole Department. We pray that you may find the wisdom and insight appropriate to the heavy responsibilities which are yours.

With utmost sincerity,

John R, Cowell, D.M.A., Professor University of Arkansas

c.c. Mr. Don Hull

Department of Adult Probation and Parole

# Letter from Ted to Edna

*Written from prison, after granted a stay of execution. Contained in envelope: 2x letters from Ted. 2x letters from Edna, returned.*

*Transcription of entire letter (1 of 2).*

Ted Bundy
Florida State Prison
Box 747
Starke, Florida
32091

August 1, 1986

Dear Edna,

Enclosed you will find a letter I wrote to you nearly six weeks ago. I didn't mail it when I finished writing it because I wasn't sure it said what I wanted it to say. So I decided to hold on to it for a while. I felt you would forgive such a delay seeing that you waited ten years to make your feelings known to me.

Well, six weeks have passed. Things have calmed down a bit. I don't feel noticeably wiser, but I am definitely older. I finally felt like it was time to take another look at the letter I wrote you, in part because I must admit it's Friday night and it came down to *Miami Vice*, *The Love Boat*, an old copy of the *Smithsonian*, or your letter. I'll read the *Smithsonian* later.

The letter I wrote you is a little long and too "preachy" in parts. It does manage to say much of what I feel needs to be said, but not all. It's an honest rendering of my thoughts, incomplete and constantly evolving though they may be.

I did purposefully avoid discussing your accusations and your proposed revelations. You did say in one of your letters that you were tired of my trying "to cover up." No sense tiring you out. Besides, I did not feel then, and don't feel now that I have to defend myself against every piece of innuendo, gossip or accusation that comes along, even from well-meaning relatives.

I won't disregard your accusations completely. I will say this much, I have not killed anyone. And this for all those who mourn: Let the dead bury the dead (Luke 9:60) for he is not a God of the dead but of the living: for all live unto him (Luke 20:38).

I don't mean this to be my final word on the subject to you. What I would like for you to do is read what I have written and what you have written and then quietly think about it. When you're ready for a calm, compassionate and loving dialogue on these things, write me. I'll be ready.

Love and peace,

ted

P.S. I've also enclosed the two letters you wrote to me.

# Letter from Ted to Edna

*Written from prison, originally unsent. Contained in envelope:
2x letters from TB. 2x letters from Edna, returned.*

*Transcription of entire letter (2 of 2)*

June 18th, 1986

Dear Edna,

Thanks for writing. I received two letters from you the first on June 5 and a second June 12. As you said, it's been the better part of ten years since I heard from you. Your letters don't reveal anything about what is happening in your life. I do hope all is going well for you and your family.

Did you receive the Christmas card I sent you? I didn't have a current address for you until your parents sent it to me around Christmas time last year.

Now, as to your letters...they do express a considerable amount of anger, bitterness and general unhappiness. I think it's good that you wrote them. It's good, if by writing them, you begin to open yourself up and honestly examine your thoughts and feelings about this whole matter.

Edna, on an intellectual, factual level of knowing, you don't know me. I am not saying that in a mean or derogatory way. You just don't know how it is for me now any more than I know how your life is for you now and what your thoughts and feelings are.

What you seem to be basing what you said in your letter on is an assortment of random recollections and a multitude of impressions which have been drawn from years of being exposed to the sensational publicity, the rumors, the gossip about some character named Ted Bundy. Well, I am not the fond memories you have of your cousin Ted, just as you are not my equally fond memories of you. Neither am I the TV news accounts, the newspaper stories, the books, the innuendos, the gossip about Ted Bundy. I am just as I am here and now. If you truly wish to be of some help, then you must dispossess yourself of all these images and know me as I am.

I certainly understand the anger and hatred you expressed. I do understand your confusion over motivations and causes. Your desire to know is natural. But you cannot know and understand me until you let go of your anger and transcend it. Anger is a barrier which divides and destroys. Just as crucial, you cannot know me until you know, truly know yourself. I hope that by expressing your anger you have begun the process of transformation through which you actually free yourself of the anger and fear.

Dear cousin, when you come to know yourself, you will know me. There is nothing that I have experienced that you have not experienced in some way. Far greater and fundamental are our similarities...far fewer and superficial our differences. When we magnify our similarities we awaken our ability to compassionately understand one another. Not by judging, analyzing, comparing and criticizing do we come to know one another, but through compassionately loving one another do we reach that place where we are one.

I can only tell you what I know and I only know a small portion of what there is to be discovered. This much I can testify to: love is the force which heals and transforms us. By studing [sic] ourselves, by listening to and being honest with ourselves we go beyond ourselves to be enlightened by all things. Being enlightened by all things we free ourselves to be guided by our true and loving nature. It's a gradual, growing process.

You'll have to excuse me. I have been rambling on. The point I am getting at is that the first and most important thing we can do for someone is to love them unconditionally and give her/him room to grow when she/he is ready. I love you not because of the good memories, or despite the bad, but because you are you. I hope that someday you can feel the same way toward me.

There is a way and the light of love reveals it to us.

Watch yourself, quiet yourself, love yourself and there's nothing you will not know. Do this and you will know me as I am, here and now.

We'll find the way.

Peace,

ted

*Don, Edna, and baby Anna.*

# Winter in a Summer Home

E ven with the little bouts of nausea during the first couple of months, I didn't see what the big deal was about pregnancy. I felt healthy, ready to take on the world.

At four months, I took a hiking trip with Pamela through the Olympics. The two of us carried packs over rough terrain deep in the backcountry for a week and slept on the ground at night. In fact, the only thing that slowed us down wasn't my condition, but instead the old pickup truck I'd borrowed from Don's brother for the trip. Practically antiquated, it had the stick shift on the column, and when I drove at any speed, the truck jerked and bumped so much that I had to wonder if the ensuing nausea I felt came from the pregnancy or the truck itself.

In 1976, Don worked for a man named Stan Harrison, a craftsman builder known widely for his custom homes. Stan preferred to bring on new apprentices who had little to no experience. He liked to train them "the right way" before they developed bad habits, then set them free after a couple years to go on to build not only stunning houses but lucrative careers.

When Don and the rest of Stan's team began work on a home on the South Head Peninsula, a little finger of land jutting into Puget Sound from Delano Bay, he knew it would be his last project with Stan. After two years of invaluable instruction, and with the prospect of supporting a new baby, it was time Don moved on.

The soon-to-be house's owner, a client from Arizona, wanted it for a summer home to escape the heat of the desert where she resided the rest of the year. She traveled to Washington a few times during construction and took a liking to Don—a common occurrence with him—who told her that we were soon expecting our first child. Since the house was set to be completed in August or September, the client had a proposition. How would Don and I like to move into the brand new, custom-built house and watch the property for her until she was ready to come early summer of next year? It would be a great place to bring home a new baby, she pitched, and we could live rent-free if Don agreed to complete the deck out back.

Needless to say, we jumped on it.

By October when we moved in, I was six months pregnant, and my earlier buoyancy had all but gone. My midsection had ballooned. The thirty pounds I'd gained by that point represented more than a quarter of my body weight, and I struggled to carry it. Walking even a few steps became a chore. I'd reached the very uncomfortable stage of late pregnancy, and after settling into the house, I was basically beached.

But no one could've asked for a better place for it. I still think back on that house as a sort of Shangri-la. From my necessarily reclined position, I'd trace the soaring cedar ceilings with my eyes as they rose at an angle, meeting clerestory windows that kept the space bathed in western light from one side, while the east wall disappeared into solid glass overlooking the bay. Built up on a high ridge, the house had a perfect view of Mount Rainier, and one of Don's and my favorite activities quickly became watching the sunrise over its peak, turning the air a fiery orange. We'd often have the window open in the mornings, and whenever we'd hear the loud slap of water splashing, we'd hurry—or hobble, in my case—over to see orcas frolicking in the water. I had a lot of empathy for whales at that time. Still, as I watched, I couldn't help but note that their movements looked a lot more graceful than mine.

The house became a perfect gathering spot for friends, even if it was off the beaten path. When my old roommates offered to throw me a baby shower, I told them we'd have to do it at the house since I couldn't go anywhere, and they weren't disappointed a bit. We hosted Thanksgiving at the house that year, too, though our friends offered to make all the food. It's a good thing. By then, my pregnancy brain had made me so spacey that when Pamela asked me to supply only one item—the rolls—it wasn't until halfway through the meal that I realized I'd completely forgotten them.

Don and I didn't have a lot of money, but we had a strong network of friends and neighbors. From them we were given just about everything a baby could ever need, much of it barely used for a few months by a neighbor's child before being outgrown. My parents helped us buy a brand-new crib, and I was in heaven setting up the house for the baby's arrival.

Even as my due date neared, Don and I hadn't settled on a name. We talked more about boys' names and felt we were zeroing in on a favorite, but we had absolutely nothing for a girl. We probably should've seen that as a sign.

\* \* \*

All through my pregnancy I tried not to think about Ted. Still reeling from the truth of what he'd done, I felt an almost physical revulsion to allowing him, even mentally, to infiltrate this period of my life, which I thought of as sacrosanct.

\* \* \*

Earlier that year on March 1, Ted had been found guilty of aggravated kidnapping after Carol DaRonch identified him in court in Utah. Up to that point he'd remained free on bail, but after the judge read his conviction, guards cuffed Ted and locked him behind bars.

In October while Don and I settled into house-sitting his client's beautiful home on the peninsula, Ted lived in a small concrete box in the Utah State Prison, much less satisfied with his accommodations. That month, a warden found Ted hiding in the bushes of the prison yard. On him, Ted carried a smuggled go-bag with things obviously intended to aid a prison escape: new identification documents, road maps, and airline schedules.

It was around this time that Don and I packed a go-bag ourselves— though a very different sort—to have on hand whenever the time came to rush to the hospital.

A few days following Ted's thwarted escape plan, he was formally charged with the murder of Caryn Campbell in Colorado, who'd disappeared while on a ski trip with her fiancé and his children the previous year. Police had scoured Ted's Volkswagen, the same one I'd ridden in multiple times, and found hairs that they determined to match three women, one of whom being Caryn. Plans were made for Ted to be extradited to Colorado to await trial.

Things were unraveling fast around him. While Ted's future closed in tighter and tighter, I watched the calendar and knew mine was opening up in new and joyous ways.

\* \* \*

In late December, my due date came and went.

\* \* \*

On New Year's Eve, two locals named Rufus and Biz (they were brother and sister) planned to throw a big bonfire party at the tip of the South Head peninsula where their family owned property. It promised to be an unforgettable bash to ring in 1977. I loved beach bonfires, where the salty logs and driftwood often turned the flames an otherworldly blue. But at that point, I was already a week late and in so much discomfort, nothing could get me out of the house.

Or, almost nothing.

Sometime that afternoon, I felt a snap in my uterus. Being overdue, I had an inkling my water had broken, and luckily I managed to rush to the bathroom before making a mess.

It was there that the first contraction started. *If this is just the beginning,* I remember thinking, *and it's considered mild, then this is not going to be fun.*

Don was at work, so I went about the task of trying to track him down—not easy in the days before cell phones—but I figured we had plenty of time since the contractions were still so far apart. After finally getting ahold of Clarke, he quickly agreed to run to Don's jobsite with the news.

In no time, Don rushed in the door, pale but excited, looking like a big kid himself with a grin on his face. He began rushing to get things ready, though we already had the go-bag packed, and I could see how grubby he was from the construction site. I assured him we still had time—I'd been timing my contractions—and he should take a shower while he still had the chance. The shower he took was so fast, I'm surprised the water had time to hit him before he jumped out again.

The nearest hospital was an hour's drive away in Tacoma, and though still too early to head to labor and delivery, we decided we wanted to be closer when labor hit. My brother's apartment offered us the perfect solution, being only five minutes from the hospital. We set a plan to go there and wait until showtime.

Anxious to get moving, we grabbed the go-bag and hopped in the car. I'd bought the red 1967 Cadillac Coupe deVille convertible with some of my proceeds from working in Alaska as a sort of consolation gift. God, I loved driving that car. But under the circumstances, Don insisted he drive, and though his nerves made him hit the accelerator, spinning the tires as we peeled out from the driveway, I didn't even give him a look. A contraction had me too busy trying to remember how to breathe.

As we sped through the winding country roads, the contractions began getting more frequent and intense. I leaned back in my seat, gripping the plush leather I usually found so comfortable. But no matter what I did, no matter how I positioned myself, I could not get comfortable.

While we crossed the Purdy Causeway, I suddenly blurted out, "What if it's a girl?" We still hadn't come up with any ideas we liked, and now time was running out. Don, who was busy driving, said the first thought that came to his mind. "How about Anna Marie?"

I loved it, and that was that. Don had a sister and a grandmother with the name, so it seemed an apt homage. And I simply liked the sound of

*Edna's 1967 Cadillac DeVille convertible.*

it. It just felt right. Perhaps the little girl in my belly had somehow sent us a message. Knowing now the strong, confident woman she'd grow into, it wouldn't surprise me that she'd found a way to cast her vote.

\* \* \*

We walked up and down the floors at John's place for hours, timing contractions. This was the same apartment where, only two years earlier, I'd been attacked and left bleeding between the buildings, though that was the farthest thing from my mind at the time. These new memories—full of hope and nervous excitement—helped overwrite the stigma of the old. With life changing so fast, I was determined to shut the door on the past.

For better or worse, this philosophy would govern my life for the next fifty years.

It was night when Don and I finally set off for the hospital. At midnight, though I'd begun labor, the baby still hadn't arrived when the clock ticked over from 1976 to 1977.

Out on South Head, the beach party crescendoed. With lots of good friends in attendance, I'm told there were many toasts to our new baby—an excuse to drink a little more, I'm sure. We heard later it got a bit out of hand. Intoxicated with drink and high spirits, people began taking off their clothes and throwing them into the fire. This was, after all, the age of streaking! Swept away in the moment, Rufus even threw in his watch.

By the end of the evening—a chilly one, might I add—while I heaved and sweated through a very long labor at the hospital, half the party at the beach was naked and quite drunk. They clearly had a better night than Don and I, though I can't say I'm sorry to have missed it.

\* \* \*

On the following morning, Anna Marie was born.

She was perfect, with all the important parts intact—I counted. She even came with a head full of dark hair and powerful lungs, so much so that when the nurses would bring her to me to feed, they often had smiles on their faces and tales of how she'd awakened all the other babies in the nursery.

I had no idea what to do with a baby—even holding her made me feel clumsy—but thankfully Don did. Growing up second oldest in a big Catholic family, he'd learned early how to help his mom change diapers and rock his siblings to sleep. Don loved babies, and they loved him. His mother had made us a bunch of cloth diapers, and Don patiently demonstrated to me how they worked.

Not long after, we switched to Pampers.

Bringing Anna home to the light-filled house was a dream come true. We put the crib in our room, not far from my side of the bed, and I'd watch her for hours.

Somewhere in my haze of happiness, I broke my own rule of mental insulation and thought about the mothers of the women Ted had murdered. They'd brought their baby girls home, too, at one point. What I felt for Anna seemed incomparable to me, so big I thought I'd burst, but I knew they'd felt it for their daughters as well.

Tears streamed down my face. As I stared at Anna, Ted's crimes took on a whole new meaning.

*Ted can never meet her*, I thought. *No matter what, I have to keep her safe.*

# Letter from Edna to Ted in Prison

*Written after finally receiving response from Ted.*

*Transcription of entire letter.*

August 8, 1986

Dear Ted,

I was most gratified that you did write. I had my doubts that you would respond. Especially with the tremendous tension you must have been undergoing last month. I have very strong feelings about the death penalty...state sanctioned murder. Enough on that subject.

Your letter was interesting. I acknowledge that the past is over. We are what we are today and, of course, not 10 years ago. All that is true, Ted. However, no matter how hard you try to disconnect the past from the present you will surely fail. They are linked together. You are responsible for what you did in the past just as I am responsible for my actions in the past. If I had cut my arm off 10 years ago it would still be gone today. Certainly, I would have adapted...proceeded with my life...but I would always be suffering the consequences. Ted, I majored in History at the UW. The past helps shape the future. We can learn from the past. We build on experiences. Scientists benefit from previous discoveries and expand on them. No matter how hard you try to wipe it out, the past will not go away.

Now, if this gives you the impression that I dwell in the past, then the point has been missed. I look to the future...always have. However, we all must be accountable for what we do now. You discuss love, forgiveness...knowing yourself. I am not a hysterical, emotional, unpredictable female. Surprise. I think about a lot of things and am not the type to be impetuous. Those letters I sent you were an exercise at being direct, Ted, which you seem to have a hard time doing. Your cover letter was more in touch. Your first letters told me little about you. I've heard the "Know thyself and you will know me" stuff.

Ted, you have got layers and layers of STUFF to pull off. I want to hear your soul talking...what you are thinking. Good heavens, how could you have gotten so terribly in trouble if you didn't kill someone? Sorry, you haven't given me enough.

Ted, I will always love you...that is not what is at stake here. Peace love. Yuk. Those are too important to bandy about—to use. We all have the capacity to forgive too...that will come later. I am asking you not to run away from your past. You have your back to it right now but that will not make it go away. It is coming up behind you relentlessly.

Turn around and take a peek at it. Just a quick one. I think facing it head on all at once would slam you against the wall with bone crushing force.

We all have a tremendous amount of power. It is how we choose to use that power that is the key. I am powerful—extremely powerful...I could use that power any number of ways. Ted, you have power—now what do you do with it?

You quote Luke—let the dead bury the dead—this is not a war—these are not faceless people. Fine, they should turn their backs on the past and live for the present—is that what you are saying? We are the sum total of all of our life's experiences. You are too, Ted. Guess what—you can't get rid of it...I cannot discard who I was 10 years ago. I certainly have evolved during that time period but essentially you will find very familiar parts of me still intact.

Is it possible for you to write about straight facts? Can you do that? You say I am totally bamboozled by the media. Well, here is your chance. I want to hear...read...your side. I will listen. You were right about being preachy. You aren't the only one guilty of that. However, you aren't going to get any false messages from me. I am not covering up anything.

Tell me about the past

Tell me the truth

On another note—yes, I got your Christmas card. I noted that it sounded like everything was hunky-dory...I want to know what your days are like, what you eat, what you read, what you feel when you are struggling to survive. I want substance, not gossamer on butterfly wings!

Now—you wanted to hear a little about me—us—my family. (By the way, I'd like you to do the same.)

Don and I just celebrated our 10th wedding anniversary. Our daughter, Anna, is 9 years old. She loves to swim and is darn good at it. My parents live down the beach from us and Anna stays with them before and after school. She is learning how to play the piano from my dad. Boy, she is lucky!

I work for an advertising/publishing company. I have been with them for nearly 3 years. I work with hotels, restaurants, major league sports and the theatre. It is an exciting and challenging job. As a matter of fact, I have been involved in one type of sales job or another for the past six years. I like to negotiate, set my own schedule and make as much money from my skills as I feel like. I've met local celebrities and know a lot of interesting people. I am an on-the-road type person. Sitting in an office all day is not my cup of tea. My husband, Don, is a superintendent for a construction firm. He runs about 20 jobs at once and is half crazed keeping up with all the details. Some days he loves it, other days he wonders.

We occasionally go to the opera (dad's influence) but prefer to take off in our little boat...or go up to Whidbey Island and dream about owning a little shack on the beach.

John got married to a Philadelphia girl in May...in fact he lives in Phil. He works for a securities firm and is buying a house. He seems to have returned to the native land.

Do you remember Aunt Ginny? Of course, you do. She's arriving here this evening for a couple of weeks. Her husband, Ed, just died last week.

Oh, a final note about anger. You bet I am angry. It doesn't control me, though. It is an outlet. I get angry when people abuse and when they allow themselves to be abused. But, most of all, I get angry when people find a thousand reasons or excuses for what they did but do not take responsibility for those actions. I use my anger to become powerful. I can think back on scores of times when I have used my anger to create very positive change. It gets me motivated.

Well, Don is trying to talk to me...he's accusing me of being too pre-occupied with this letter. He wants to boogy! So, I must bid you adieu. Hope you can piece together all my thoughts.

Until later, dear cousin,

Edna

*Don and baby Anna in trailer home.*

# Escape

The phone rattled in the small trailer. Leaving Anna propped safely on the carpet in the living room, I pulled myself to my feet and made the short trip to the phone.

After our house-sitting arrangement at the beautiful custom home on the peninsula ended, Don and I had been sorry to leave. The feeling only deepened when the reality of what we could afford manifested in the form of a very modest mobile home a few miles away in a place called Home, Washington. Here in the woods, we had no views and no way to do laundry, which infant babies make a lot of. I became very familiar with the local laundromat.

As if to make the trailer feel even smaller, Anna had just started walking. I'd personally crawled over every inch of that trailer, on elbows and knees, to rid it of all hazards, and when the holiday season approached, we'd placed the Christmas tree up high where her little hands couldn't reach.

Brushing fallen needles from my knees, I pulled off the phone receiver and put it to my ear.

"Hi, Edna?" I recognized the voice immediately.

Ted.

With my heart rate spiking, I kept one eye trained on Anna, for once grateful for the trailer's small size where she couldn't leave my sight.

He was calling me from the jail phone in Colorado. I could hear his smile as he told me how happy he was to have gotten ahold of me.

I didn't know how to respond. In truth, I had no idea what my relationship with Ted was anymore, or what I even wanted it to be. By then he'd been extradited from Utah to the jail in Garfield County, Colorado, where he was awaiting trial for the murder of Caryn Campbell.

Ted represented a gaping wound in my life, one I still didn't know how to heal. I'd seen a side of him that made me understand he was capable of the horrors of which he'd been accused. If I was honest with myself, I was terrified of him. But somehow that didn't erase the history Ted and I shared, nor the love I'd had for the person he'd been. Love doesn't just disappear. And since I hadn't known how to properly process it—or if that was even possible—it remained like a lump in my throat.

This is the lump I tried to swallow as I listened to him speak. His voice sounded both familiar and strange. He spoke to me the same way he'd spoken to me during family beach days in Longbranch, impromptu strolls in the park in Seattle, or shared dinners at my apartment, and it was difficult not to slip back into our old dynamic.

But it wasn't the same. He was phoning me from jail, for one thing. This was the first time we'd spoken since he'd been out on bail in December of 1975, when I'd dragged him away from the street corner where he'd drawn a crowd. Now it was December 30, 1977. I wished, then, that sometime in those two years I'd had the forethought to consider the possibility that we'd speak again. Maybe I'd have figured out what to say.

Settling on a default politeness, I asked Ted questions about himself and what it was like in jail. That got him going. "Jail's no fun," he said, understating for impact. Impassioned, he told me how much he hated it there, how he longed for the freedom he used to have. His rant quickly led to him reassuring me—or more likely himself—that the state didn't have a case against him, but the juries in Colorado were biased.

I didn't know how to respond to any of this. We didn't get newspapers delivered to us out there in the country, so I wasn't up to date on the details of the trial. Instead, I just let him talk, keeping an eye on Anna.

"So," Ted said, "what would you think if I got out of here?"

That got my attention. Something told me he wasn't referring to winning his case. Sensing that clarification was needed, he went on.

"If I escaped."

I was certain he was teasing me in some misguided effort to reboot our old playful dynamic, and that made me angry. The truth was, he'd escaped from jail already once before, jumping from the second story window of the law library where he'd been granted access since he was serving as his own attorney. Ted had been injured, sleep-deprived, and half-frozen when he was caught after six days, after living rough in the mountains. Absolutely nothing about the idea had been good.

By proposing a second escape to me on a phone line certainly monitored by guards, I didn't think it possible he actually meant it. Surely after his first escape, he was now locked down under maximum security, and I thought it likely he was using this phone call to blow off steam and rankle his captors. To be honest, I felt used. I sensed this was a dark game he played, teasing not only me but the guards listening in on our phone call, and I resented being dragged into it.

Later I learned Ted had been given use of a phone card at the jail, a special permission granted because he was a member of his own legal team. This phone card meant his calls couldn't be listened to by the guards.

But I didn't know that at the time.

I heard my voice change, instantly exhausted, as I responded. "That would be a big mistake, Ted," I said, deciding my role in his dark game was the voice of reason. I reminded him how bad of an idea it had been last time. And if he truly believed the state didn't have a strong enough case against him, wouldn't it be better to simply wait for the trial? "Just don't do it," I emphasized while trying to rub away a blooming headache.

Maybe Ted wasn't happy with my response. I thought I'd heard just about everything from him in the short phone call, but he had one more bombshell.

"I shouldn't even be the one in here," he complained. "John's always been the weird one."

That was it. My patience had run dry. I was furious.

*John's the weird one?* As if that was a crime. As if being different measured anywhere in the ballpark of what Ted had done.

Sure, my brother marched to the beat of his own drum. Growing up with him, I knew it better than most. But he was brilliant. He had meaningful jobs and contributed to society. He attracted wonderful, smart, confident women who loved him. Didn't that say something?

Most importantly, John was a good person.

I thought back to two years previous when the allegations had first emerged, back before those of us who knew Ted personally could get anywhere near believing them. Ted had been like a brother to John, so when the police came knocking, asking that John help them investigate Ted, John at first refused. He didn't believe Ted was guilty then, and his first instinct was to remain loyal to his cousin.

I wondered then if Ted would have shown John the same allegiance.

But there was something else about Ted's comment that struck a bad chord.

At certain times during the past, I'd wondered if Ted liked to fancy himself a member of our family. The way he went out of his way to introduce his girlfriend to my parents, the subtle way he stood next to us during that memorable family picture. I hadn't minded as a kid. In fact, I'd liked thinking of Ted as another brother.

But Ted's comment that John was "the weird one" betrayed a feeling that Ted thought he was better than John. I felt repulsed.

And I wouldn't stand for it.

"You're saying *John* is the weird one, Ted?" I snapped. "John's a good person!"

Shortly after that, the conversation wrapped up. I didn't want to be dragged into any more of Ted's wild notions, and Ted had either run out of allotted phone time or interest.

❋ ❋ ❋

Two days later, on New Year's Day, we were awakened in the morning by a knock at the door that shook the entire trailer.

I sat up in bed as Don stirred. It was a holiday, and we'd looked forward to sleeping in, but the sky outside was still dark. I tried to clear my head.

Another knock concussed the flimsy door.

Don stumbled out of bed, telling me to wait there while he dealt with whatever was needed.

But something was wrong; I could sense it. Quickly getting out of bed, I padded to the small hallway and put my ear to the closed door next to ours. I listened.

Nothing. No cries. No fussing. Anna was still asleep.

Down the hall, I could make out more than one male voice talking with Don, but the words were indistinct. Then three consonants stuck out, and I heard them clear as day.

*FBI.*

\* \* \*

I joined Don at the door to find two agents standing outside.

Ted, they informed us, had escaped from jail two nights before. They'd only discovered he was gone the day previous.

*So he actually meant it*, was my first thought. Don and I shared a look that spoke of so many emotions it's impossible to list them all. Glancing back towards the hallway to Anna's room, I motioned the men outside. I told them we had an infant baby inside sleeping. In politeness, they asked how old she was.

"One," Don said, and before he could stop himself, added, "today." The morning when the FBI showed up happened to be Anna's first birthday.

In a jarring moment of unreality, the FBI agents offered their well-wishes and then kindly kept their voices low for the rest of the conversation.

They said Ted had been starving himself for weeks, shrinking down his already thin frame, so he could slip out a hole he'd ripped in the ceiling of his cell hidden by a light fixture. He'd chosen the night of December 30 strategically because so many workers at the jail were out for the holidays. After shimmying up through the hole, he'd stolen some clothes from the apartment of one of the jailers before he walked right out the front door.

The agents had come, they said, because they knew Ted had called me the afternoon before he escaped.

On cue, I began replaying the conversation in my head. Did I say something that Ted could have misconstrued? I didn't see how I could have been any clearer.

The agents began to tell us, in detail, the trouble we'd be in if we aided and abetted a fugitive. Their tone wasn't exactly threatening, but they left no doubt they were very serious as they laid out the facts.

But Don didn't let them finish. "I can assure you we have no intention of helping Ted," he interrupted.

One of the agents reminded us that Ted had called me only hours before he escaped. He was on the run and looking for somewhere safe. I think that's when the danger fully dawned on us.

*Ted might come here.*

Immediately, I could feel the anger emanating off Don in waves. He looked the lawmen straight in the eye and promised that if Ted showed up, he'd do whatever was necessary to protect his family. "Even," he said, "if I have to fight him to the death."

The agents handed us their cards, and we promised we'd be in contact if we had any news. Then, busy with the task of finding a fugitive, they left us on our own.

\* \* \*

That day we dressed Anna in her warmest coat and took off. I don't remember where we went. It didn't matter. We knew we couldn't stand being there at the trailer, wondering if anyone would show up.

Not anyone. Ted.

Where could he be going?

I hated to admit it, but our place seemed as likely as anywhere. Back in Seattle, Ted used to love dropping by unannounced. And neither Don nor I could shake the significance that he'd called me the day he escaped. That seemed important. Hell, the FBI agreed.

"He knew we wouldn't believe him," Don said, furious. "He called on purpose. I don't know what his message was, but it sure as hell wasn't benign."

Ted would be desperate. That was certain. What was he capable of in his desperation?

If he wanted us to hide him, we'd absolutely refuse. I couldn't stomach the thought of letting Ted into my home. I pictured him in that tiny trailer, standing by Anna's crib, and I shuddered.

So when we refused him, how would he respond? He couldn't just leave then, not in a million years. He wouldn't have anywhere else to go. And worse, I was certain he wouldn't want to take the risk that we'd call the police and give up his location.

Would Ted take us hostage? Don promised it would never get that far. "I'll attack him first," he said. "I won't even let him talk." My immediate thought was, *Okay, but what if you aren't home when he comes?*

Would Ted kill us?

Assuming Don was home, he wouldn't go down without a fight—he'd made that clear. And Don was strong, in peak physical condition from all the labor he'd been doing. But Ted was cunning.

What if he managed to hurt Don?

What if he killed Don?

Through the day, with these thoughts screaming in our minds, Don and I fought to stay calm, keeping on happy faces for Anna. We had to pretend we weren't scared out of our minds.

\* \* \*

When we returned late that afternoon, it was already growing dark. I held Anna while Don checked the property. There were no signs of forced entry. No signs anyone had been there at all.

We entered through the thin, aluminum door. The trailer had never felt so small; the wilderness outside—with all it might be hiding—had never felt so big.

Every sound seemed magnified. The wind through the leaves, a snap of a twig—each noise echoed, dangerous and horrible. I tried to put on music to drown it out, but the idea that we might not hear something approaching was worse. I quickly turned it off.

\* \* \*

Don went outside to his pickup and rifled through some construction gear until he found a couple of two-by-fours.

While I made a cake in the tiny kitchen with Anna on my hip, I kept one eye on Don as he lugged his tools from the truck and, in the day's dying light, carefully cut the two-by-fours down to size, measuring them repeatedly. Finally satisfied, he locked his tools back in the truck and carried the freshly cut boards inside.

As I watched, Don lined up the first two-by-four and pushed it tight along the bottom of the door. Then bracing the second two-by-four perpendicular to the first, he placed it across the trailer's width and pressed hard, wedging it firmly against a built-in lower cabinet. A perfect fortification.

"Nobody's getting in now," he said.

Anna crawled from my arms to where her father stood. He picked her up and held her close. "Now, let's celebrate somebody's birthday."

\* \* \*

I'd never given Anna sugar before, but I wanted to make the day special for her. Babies are so perceptive. I didn't want her to absorb our anxiety, to pick up on how jumpy her parents had become. I wanted it to be a happy occasion.

That night, Don and I sang to her, and I lit a single candle. She loved the candle, eyes aglow as we helped her blow it out.

I spooned cake into her mouth, her first taste of real sugar.

Instantly a mixture of disgust and betrayal crossed her face, and she spit it out.

After all the tension, Don and I looked at each other, and we burst out laughing.

\* \* \*

After putting Anna to bed, I found Don again at the door, jamming a chair under the handle, so it couldn't be forced open. More importantly, he said, the chair braced the middle of the flimsy door. One more line of defense.

As I got ready for bed, I could hear drawers opening and closing from the kitchen. Then Don appeared holding a large butcher knife, which he placed next to our bed. "Just in case," he said.

He told me he'd left another knife behind the toilet, and I made a mental note to make sure they were all out of Anna's reach by the morning. Don told me of other tools—his framing hammer, his father's ax—that he'd placed strategically around the property if he needed a weapon. I understood this was important to him. He wanted to be prepared for anything.

Still, neither of us slept that night. We listened to the night sounds of the woods, to the soft stirring of Anna from the other side of the wall. "Nobody's getting in," I reminded Don, and he nodded.

"And if he does," he said, "I'll be ready."

\* \* \*

As the days progressed, we tried to convince ourselves that the odds he'd show up grew less and less likely. But then we'd be visited by another wave of law enforcement, coming by to check on us, and the fear would ratchet up again.

After the FBI, our little trailer was also visited first by a pair of local detectives, then by the Washington State Patrol. We were officially people of interest.

The nice thing about these visits was it gave us an opportunity to receive updates and to ask a million questions. Since Ted's escape, either Don or I were sure to grab a copy of the *Seattle Times* from the local country store every day. We'd devour every word written about him, but we still hungered for more details.

The answers we got from the different officers did nothing to allay our fears. We learned details of the investigation into Ted with other murders he was suspected of in at least four states. The officers all wanted to drive home the fact that Ted was dangerous, and it wouldn't be a good idea to let him inside.

Each time, we reassured the officers that we'd be in contact immediately if we had any communication from Ted.

Each night before bed, Don would secure the two-by-fours, wedging us in tight.

❊ ❊ ❊

It wasn't long before Don had to return to work. This meant I'd be all alone with Anna during the day. Ted was still at large, and the police had no leads on his location.

No way in hell was I staying at the trailer.

I contacted our friends, Clarke and Ann. Without thinking twice, they told me to grab Anna and spend the day with them.

So it was that this became my routine. Every morning as soon as I'd kissed Don goodbye, I'd pack up Anna's things for the day, and the two of us would flee to the Longbranch dock, where Clarke and Ann kept their boat. In those days they lived on a Grand Banks Trawler called *The Lesson #1*, a beautiful wooden boat with a warm, mahogany inner cabin. This boat became my safe haven.

My escape.

We'd cast off and spend our days cruising around Filucy Bay. Or sometimes we'd go past the lighthouse point towards Anderson or McNeil Island and back. It didn't matter where we went, as long as we stayed on the water.

Gone were the snapping branches, the rustling leaves, the dark shadows that plagued me on land.

Out on the water, I could breathe.

No one could get to us there, not without making a commotion. Day after day, the water offered us protection, and we were utterly surrounded by it. It lapped reassuringly at the boat from all sides, rocking us like a lullaby.

From the boat, I could survey the shore. Ted was out there, somewhere on land. But sitting on the deck, the land looked small and distant.

Out on the water, we were safe.

# Letter from Ted to Edna

*Response to her previous letter.*

*Transcription of entire letter.*

November 13, 1986

Dear Edna,

I came across your last letter (August 8) recently. Excuse me for not writing sooner.

I don't believe I have the time right now to properly respond to the issues raised in your letter. I imagine that books have and could be written on the relevancy and the nature of the past and how it relates to the present and future. Beyond that, your request that I tell you about the past could cover a few volumes, even if I was inclined to do so.

Anyway, I wanted to write to let you know I appreciated your letter, even though I see things differently on a number of points you raised.

I'll attempt to summarize a response to your letter.

1. I take full responsibility for all that I have done. I have no problem with that.

2. Yes, and I agree that we must learn from what has occurred in the so-called past. It's essential. The way I see it, that's the true value of reviewing the past: to learn from it, to grow, to change, to be transformed.

3. You wrote, "I've heard the know thyself and you will know me stuff." You sounded skeptical. So we disagree. I have discovered that only by studying myself can I transcend myself to know others, to be enlightened by all things. That doesn't mean you can't see it another way.

4. "Peace/love...yuk," you wrote. "Those are too important to bandy about, to use." Again, I agree. I wasn't bandying about or using those words, and I am happy to know you wouldn't.

5. "I am asking you not to run away from your past," you said. Okay. Well, I won't. I promise, and I haven't been. That which I call the past isn't something I fear. I have no guilt, remorse or regret over anything I've done. What's done is done. The important thing to do is to learn from it in such a way that this new awareness becomes a part of my life

here and now, or to put it another way, that I don't make the same mistakes.

6. "Is it possible for you to write about straight facts? Can you do that," you asked?

Yes.

7. "Tell me the truth."

I have. I will.

So where do we go from here?

I'd be happy for us to get to know each other as we are now. In the course of that I have no problem with discussing that which is referred to as the past. But I have no interest, need or desire to engage in some epic recount. I have enough to do, enough to think and write about just by concerning myself with what's happening in my life today.

After being out of touch for ten years, you rush in out of the blue and begin demanding I tell you this and that, making all sorts of accusations and jumping to all sorts of conclusions about me in the process. I was glad to hear from you, don't get me wrong, but no one appoints you inquisitor or prosecutor. I'm under no obligation to "prove myself" to anyone. All I'm saying is to take it easy, Edna. I don't need a hard sell approach. How would you feel if someone came to you insisting that you reveal the intimate details of your life and making derogatory remarks about your character?

I don't know you and I don't pretend to. I'd like to but I'm certainly not going to demand "your side" or "about the past" or "the truth." Be yourself, Edna. I love you the way you are. I would like the same consideration.

What's life like here?

I live in a 9x12 foot space. There is a bunk and toilet and sink. We're down to basics here. It's like most everything the experience of being in prison can liberate or entrapped [sic]. Ghandi found his jail experiences to be uplifting, humbling. I'm stripped of so many things and being thus deprived I am free to see myself as I was not able to before.

I was awakened at 5:30 a.m. for a breakfast of cold scrambled eggs, grits, white bread, milk.

# Escape

I walked for a few hours, then sat down and started writing letters.

I'm in the cell all day. Sometimes I run back-and-forth and do sit ups and other exercises. Sometimes yoga. I usually take a nap around noon. I sleep well.

I have a small radio and TV but I don't use them much. I listen to the news on the radio ("All Things Considered"). I watch sports on TV.

Sure, it can be an unpleasant existence. I'd rather not be here but I make the most of it while I'm here. I am certainly not going to make it harder on myself than it is already. Yes, occasionally, I despair, become frustrated, angry. But generally I have a positive outlook.

I take care of myself. I eat right, exercise regularly, don't smoke, drink coffee or use drugs. I care about myself. I like myself (under the circumstances, I'd better.)

There is always something for me to do. Unlike many of my comrades, I'm never bored. There's always something to read or someone to write. I can always walk or run or work out.

Right now I'm in a special "death watch" cell near the execution chamber. I'll be here until I get a stay of execution next week. Then I'll be returned to a regular death row cell where conditions are somewhat less restrictive.

This is the third time in nine months a death warrant has been signed against me. I guess I've gotten accustomed to living with such a threat. It's no fun, but I feel very calm.

My wife and daughter are living in Seattle now. Carole had to return to Seattle to care for her mother who was severely injured in a car accident. Carole has fallen back in love with the P.N.W. (you know how it is to return), and Rosa, who was born in Florida, acclimated herself without difficulty and is thriving on, among other things working in her Grandma's garden, going to ballet class, and touring the zoo and aquarium. I think she's a genetic Puget Sounder. (She just turned five.)

Sounds like you and Don are doing great. It's good that your mom and dad are back in Seattle and close by, especially good for Anna.

Be good.

I love you.

ted

-4-

"your past", you said.
Okay. Well, I won't, I promise,
and I haven't been. That which you
call the past isn't something
I fear. I have no guilt,
remorse or regret over anything I've done. Whats done
is done. The important thing
is to learn from it in such
a way that this new awareness
becomes a part of my life
here and now, or to put it
another way, that I don't make
the same mistakes.

6. "Is it possible for you to
write about straight facts?
Can you do that", you asked?
Yes.

7. "Tell me the truth."
I have. I will.


Be good.
I love you.
Ted

# Why Florida

For over forty days, Ted remained at large.

During this time, my brother and I spoke regularly. I learned that on the day Ted called me from jail—before escaping that night—he'd also called John.

Like me, Ted had told him he was thinking of escaping. Like me, John didn't think he could possibly be serious and told him it was a bad idea. But John said that Ted had something else on his mind during their call. Ted had asked John which states were "worst for the death penalty."

My brother, with his encyclopedic mind, didn't think to ask why. Instead John simply thought about it for a moment, then he gave Ted an answer. "Probably Texas," John said. "Or Florida."

On the morning of February 15, 1978, Ted finally resurfaced.

It was in Florida.

\* \* \*

Exactly one month before, in the early hours of Sunday, January 15, an intruder broke into the Chi Omega house near Florida State University in Tallahassee. With ruthless precision, the man made his way through the bedrooms, brutally attacking and violating the women who slept in their beds. All were intended to die.

First was Margaret Bowman. They say she never woke up.

Next was Lisa Levy. At one point—I don't know if it was before or after she died—the intruder bit Lisa so hard, the bite mark was found by the medical examiner and later used in court as a form of identification, a controversial alternative to fingerprinting later deemed unreliable.

Further down the hall, the intruder attacked roommates Kathy Kleiner and Karen Chandler. With a piece of firewood stolen from downstairs, the man bashed the sleeping women over their heads hard enough to kill them. Before he could confirm they were dead, a light—possibly from next door—shone through the window.

Spooked, the man fled.

Somehow Kathy Kleiner and Karen Chandler survived.

All of this took place within fifteen minutes.

After the police arrived at the crime scene, they'd barely begun to get to work when another call came in over the radio. Only six blocks away, Cheryl Thomas was lying unconscious in a pool of blood when police found her minutes later.

No way could this be the same guy, they said. Not so soon. Not so nearby. Who would do that?

Almost a month later, Kimberly Leach disappeared from her school in Lake City, Florida.

She was twelve years old.

\* \* \*

On February 15, a mystery man was brought into custody in Pensacola after attacking the police officer who pulled him over for driving a stolen vehicle—a Volkswagen Beetle that had gone missing near the fateful Chi Omega Sorority House back in Tallahassee.

The car wasn't the only thing that had been stolen. The man also had a number of IDs and credit cards, and for days he wouldn't give Pensacola police his real name.

When they finally learned who he was, that was it for him.

Ted would never step foot outside of a prison again.

\* \* \*

When the news of Ted's capture reached us in Washington, sickened by his rampage, we could finally end our hyper-vigilance.

\* \* \*

I've had a lot of time to speculate why Ted went to Florida.

To square it with the Ted I thought I knew, my instinct says he chose Florida because it was the farthest away he could get within the contiguous United States, especially when comparing his home state of Washington. And he wanted a fresh start.

This makes sense, really. He'd accomplished the impossible by breaking out of prison and getting away with it. In those days, police departments didn't really communicate with each other, especially over state lines. Local news didn't travel much, either, instead remaining relatively contained to the area where it occurred. With a name change and a decent cover story, not to mention a knack at deception, a person could reasonably hope to get away with becoming someone new.

Ted had burned his bridges in the Northwest. Perhaps he thought his only chance lay in the Southeast.

After all, breaking out of prison required a lot of work. Who knows how long he'd had to starve himself in order to fit through the hole he'd carved in the ceiling, or what lengths he'd had to go to in order to travel so far? Why else would he go to all this trouble except to start fresh?

Yet there would be no fresh start for Ted. In Florida, his rampage was entirely different from his past crimes, so uncharacteristically unstructured, it appears he lost control completely.

I see this as proof that he lost the battle, provoked by his new freedom. The demons finally took over completely, and Ted's violent frenzy signifies his utter surrender to the beast.

He failed, and he took more innocent lives along the way.

When he refused to give the police his real identity, maybe he wasn't ready yet to admit defeat, to relinquish the future he'd hoped to construct under a new name.

Then I recall that look of disorientation on his face, that dawn of shame as self-awareness caught up to him after dancing, stoned, on my coffee table. Perhaps it's possible, after losing himself so entirely to darkness, when police asked Ted his identity he simply didn't know anymore.

\* \* \*

But what about that phone call to John when he asked about the death penalty? That Ted took off for Florida the very night John gave Florida as an answer seems too coincidental not to be important.

But what could it mean?

John believes it shows Ted had a death wish. He thinks Ted was courting his own doom in the form of the electric chair.

I know Ted hated prison. I also know he loved attention and control. In his unbalanced mind, could it be possible Ted saw Florida as a solution?

I can believe that he preferred a death sentence to a life sentence.

Why else did he act so recklessly? Why else did he stay in the neighborhood after his attacks at the Chi Omega house, to strike again that very night?

Why else, in the weeks that followed, didn't he flee the state?

To be convicted in Florida, Ted could control his own death. He must have known his execution would be national news. He likely figured it would dominate the airwaves and newsstands for weeks when it happened.

He probably relished the possibility that we'd still be talking about it decades later.

Taken in this light, Ted's Florida rampage looks different, though in no way less horrible. When Ted appeared so unhinged, so out of control, it's possible he was only acting according to plan. His frenzy may have been as much a ruse as the wearing of a sling had been, in his earlier crimes.

But if John's right and Ted intended to get caught in Florida in a manner sensational enough to land him on death row, how far did his scheming really go? What was rampage, and what was performance?

Had he been in control of himself when he bit into the flesh of Lisa Levy?

Just how calculated was his murder of twelve-year-old Kimberly Leach?

\* \* \*

After many years of trying to make sense of Ted's actions, I've come to find the endeavor futile.

There is no sense in something so senseless.

# Letter from Edna to Ted in Prison

*Response to his previous letter.*

*Transcription of entire letter.*

12/5/86

Dear Ted,

I have finally come to realize that you are what you are...I guess I thought I might be able to elicit something out of your soul...some insight and information about your past. I realize that that was probably a naive supposition.

I imagine that the shock that I was in just finally manifested itself...in the letter form. Ted, I had to at least try to find out what was in you that was so different from the Ted I knew. I felt incredibly let down and deceived... and very scared. I really thought I knew you, as well as a family member could and therefore trusted you unconditionally...yes, I loved you unconditionally. I don't know what I feel now—I still care about you a great deal. There is just so much I do not understand.

Nevertheless, I will continue to write to you but will back off from accusations. You were remarkably patient...quite surprising, in fact. I am glad you wrote. I wish that some day we could just let our hair down and talk...no walls, no defenses. I imagine you would like to be out from behind all those walls or would you? Things have changed a lot since you went in. It can be dangerous to be free.

Ted, have you been to Orcas Island? We went to visit friends there for Thanksgiving. Our friend, Clarke, commutes ever day to Decatur Island by speedboat. He and a crew of guys are building "spec" houses on the various San Juan Islands. All of the houses are worth hundreds of thousands of dollars—several hang off of cliffs commanding spectacular views of the Olympics and neighboring Islands. Last month there was a great deal of fog. You remember what it is like in the early fall—cold and warm air mix—inversions keep the cold air down on the ground producing bone chilling fog. It was like pea soup for several weeks. On a Tuesday Clarke and his crew set out for the 45-minute ride to Decatur— they kicked off at 4 pm noticing a cloud bank heading their way. They sped westward to Orcas only to be overcome after 15 minutes by an impenetrable wall of whiteness. They became disoriented and lost their way. As it became dark, they began to feel afraid. They saw a beacon and headed towards it only to find it was a sailboat at anchor with a lone running light on the port beam. They continued with one person on the bow watching out for rocks. An hour later they spotted another light. When they got right up next to it, they discovered to their dismay that it was the same boat. They had gone in a big circle. This story has a happy ending—the fog never lifted but they groped their way to Shaw Island. They had a friend who had a friend who had a cabin—they made it. Around 11:00 pm they caught a ferry to Orcas to be reunited with their anxious wives only to get up at dawn the following morning to face the fog again.

Of course, I face a different type of challenge every day. I commute from Alki Beach to Bellevue across the dreaded floating bridges. I see my life flashing before my eyes much too frequently. I wish I had a car equipped with giant bumpers, machine guns and oil slick dispensers. Boy, would I have a great time!

I will sign off with a final comment. I am appalled with what the death penalty has come to signify to our country. People are terrified and are tired of being victims. To them, killing is a just deserve [sic]—but what it does is accomplish a lot of the wrong things. It gives the state the right to commit murder. The government isn't exactly a paragon of virtue. I don't like them having their finger on the switch. Secondly, it is incredibly expensive. Look at your situation. You have been appealing the process for years at great cost to everyone. Thirdly, it makes the person awaiting the death sentence a focus of tremendous media attention. Some of them even have books and movies produced of their lives. Someone is making big bucks off of terribly unfortunate circumstances. And, finally, it is terrible for families of the victims, of the death row inmate, for the person on death row, for the public in general. The whole thing is incredible! There are some pretty horrible crimes being committed right now—they deserve major punishment...but to do it this way is all wrong. I do not pretend to know what the answer is. I many times feel that I would like to see the perpetrators of heinous crimes killed in like fashion. Ah, the question is certainly one for debate and one I imagine you feel very strongly about. I wonder...do people who know they are going to die of an incurable disease feel the same sense of injustice? For them, life is totally out of control. Some would argue that the difference lies in the matter of choice. We have that gift of choice.

# Why Florida

Well, I must bid you adieu before I get off on one of my usual tangents. Hope this letter finds you well.

Until later,

Edna

*Edna and Anna*

# 13 Coins

By the late eighties, Don, Anna, and I had purchased a house on Beach Drive. With spectacular views of Puget Sound, the Olympic Mountains, and even Mount Rainier, it was situated on a narrow street that traced the southwestern shoreline of the Alki peninsula in West Seattle. The scenic road was one that drivers tended to take either very fast or very slow, much to the chagrin of those of us who lived in the neighborhood. It was a view we never took for granted, and when Don had time off, he'd often be found flying kites at Alki Beach Park.

It had been almost a decade since Ted had been sentenced to death by electrocution for the murders of Margaret Bowman, Lisa Levy, and Kimberly Leach. He spent those years on death row at the Raiford Prison in Starke, Florida.

During that time, Ted became a public icon, the subject of countless studies and books, which often became best-sellers. One, written by *Seattle Times* reporter Richard Larsen who'd known Ted personally during his time working in local politics, had even been made into a miniseries starring Mark Harmon as Ted, for which he received a Golden Globes nomination. The casting of Mark Harmon was telling of just how the public viewed Ted. Earlier that year, Mark Harmon had been named *People* magazine's "Sexiest Man Alive."

Of course, I knew these books and TV specials existed, but I avoided them. Every reference to his name sent a distinct shock of pain straight to my nervous system. Each mention felt like a personal attack. In fact, the more popular Ted became, the more I wanted to remain invisible.

\* \* \*

At this time, I worked for a company called Entertainment. Started by a husband and wife in Detroit, the young family struggled to meet their expenses and still budget money for any leisure activities. In talking to local restaurateurs, they learned small businesses were always worried about getting enough customers to keep their doors open. That gave them an idea.

Together, the Pottikers began putting together a coupon book that made things like dining out, travel, sporting events, and concerts more affordable to young families and generated business for local companies.

The concept took off. What started over a humble kitchen table grew rapidly in cities across the country as Entertainment expanded into new markets. They'd just opened a Seattle office when I joined the sales team in 1983. By the end of 1988, I'd been promoted to District Manager for both Seattle and Tacoma.

Our regional office consisted of about twelve people—all women except for one, the regional vice president. As a small operation, we all did a little bit of everything, and it wasn't unusual for us women to switch out our suits and heels for jeans and boots to drive forklifts and unload semi-trucks filled with pallets of glossy coupon books.

It was challenging work, never dull, but we loved it, and everyone in the office grew close. We supported each other through thick and thin, even one another's quirks. I remember having to speak with one member of my team after she began consistently showing up late for work. Seattle had recently been rocked by a few earthquakes, and she confessed to me that she'd become afraid to drive under bridges and overpasses. The route she had to go to avoid them took a lot of planning ahead and at least twice as long to drive. But it wasn't my place to judge, so I merely asked her to leave a little earlier in the mornings. She was never late again.

On another occasion, our regional manager went on vacation to England, where she met a well-known British actor. She must have had a memorable time because when she returned a week or so later, she spoke with an unmistakable British accent. After talking to her, her confused clients would call me to ask what was going on. Frankly, I had a hard time explaining it.

But her romance with the actor provided the office with juicy gossip, and when he traveled to Seattle, I even got to meet him. Too bad the romance, like her accent, didn't last.

But no matter how close we became, I still hadn't told my colleagues I was related to Ted Bundy.

I never told anyone.

* * *

Beginning in 1986, the dance began between Ted and death. I'm told it went unusually fast for a capital murder case. It felt excruciating. An execution date would be announced, Ted's lawyers would hustle to find a new strategy or legal technicality to buy time, a stay would be granted, and then the process would begin again. It went round and round like a carnival ride, the kind that made me sick.

But I admit with each delay, I felt quietly relieved. Because I hadn't become familiar with Ted's dark side, it was still the old Ted I imagined when I pictured him in his prison cell. The Ted I knew didn't deserve to die.

I wondered if that Ted ever really existed, or if he was just a facade.

I remembered how repulsed I'd been during the trials, watching Ted on television as he basked in the attention, all eyes and cameras pointed at him. The clips when he represented himself were hardest to take. Ted had strutted around like a peacock as he cross-examined witnesses—many of whom were the very people he'd traumatized. I couldn't understand how the legal system allowed him to do that, that it in fact handed him the opportunity to re-traumatize these people on the witness stand while the public sat and watched.

That was the Ted I didn't know. That was the Ted who'd been sentenced to death.

But still, I wondered, did the law have the right to kill anyone? It seemed dangerously close to murder for murder, wrong for wrong.

My feelings about the death penalty were complicated, made exponentially more so by my relation to Ted. There's no road map for how to deal with something like this. It weighed on me emotionally, but instead of therapy or counseling, I did what I thought was best at the time.

I avoided the issue completely.

Especially around Anna.

* * *

In my defense, I truly believed I was protecting my daughter. What parent wouldn't do everything necessary to shield their children from such depths of perversion? Ted had stained my life forever, and I wanted to save Anna from the same debasement.

At first, of course, it was simple. I didn't tell her about Ted because she was too young to understand. But then as she grew, the time never felt right to burden her with the truth. To me she was light and pure. Ted was darkness and filth.

So the pattern held.

I knew she had some vague idea. She'd heard grumblings through extended family—something with a cousin, something bad.

An incident occurred back in 1986, when Ted's first execution date was set. Worried that his time was running out, I wrote Ted a letter in prison after six years of estrangement, and I begged him to confess. I ached for the families of Ted's victims to have any amount of closure. When he finally wrote back, his attitude hurt me deeply, but still I felt a duty to respond and keep trying. At the time of the incident, his latest letter had arrived in the mail, but I hadn't yet brought myself to read it.

Aside from our recent correspondence, I had only one or two other letters that Ted had sent me years ago from prison. I hated them. I hated having them in my house. But I couldn't throw them out, convinced I'd be releasing some plague into the world. I couldn't help but imagine a dark presence emanating from the ink, as if Ted had imbued it with his own evil nature. I always kept his letters hidden away, in isolation where they could infect nothing.

But since the newest one had just arrived, I did something very uncharacteristic and left it sitting on the bookshelf by the front door. I didn't plan to keep it there. It was only temporary until I'd steeled myself to read it.

Anna saw it.

She was eight or nine at the time. She didn't know what it was, but for some reason it interested her. As she reached to pick it up, in my head I saw Ted's inky darkness waft into the air towards her.

I pounced. I don't remember exactly what I said to stop her, but I know I said it with a gruffness that frightened her, and she understood—with what little knowledge she had—roughly what it was.

Children are so perceptive. Even at her young age, Anna could sense the topic caused me pain, and in testament to her good heart, she avoided it just as I avoided it. I guess it was learned aversion, this behavior.

Anna stepped away from the letter. I didn't explain what it was or why I'd responded the way I did. Anna didn't ask. We simply dropped it and pretended it never happened.

* * *

At some point during Ted's appeals, after another date had been set, Ted finally allowed for something he'd never before permitted: a plea of incompetence.

All along, he'd insisted that he was perfectly sane, the picture of competence. That was a crucial part of the image he sought to project, the role he never, ever wanted to stop playing for the cameras. He must have hated the blow this plea made to his public image, but at this crucial time he didn't have many cards left to play.

His defense team brought in a psychiatrist from Yale, Dr. Dorothy Lewis, to assess Ted's upbringing and mental state. Dr. Lewis got quickly to work and began contacting members of the family.

I know she spoke with my father and my brother. Neither one could tell her anything she found useful.

Other members of the family had things to say about Ted's grandfather, Sam. He could be very mean, a bully, they said. Knowing who said them, I'm inclined to believe the allegations, though I admit I never saw any of it myself having only met Sam once or twice as a young child.

As far as what Ted may have said to Dr. Lewis, I take it with a grain of salt. He had an agenda—one his life depended on—and a remarkable talent for deception.

When Dr. Lewis deemed Ted mentally incompetent, I can only wonder how Ted felt. Was it a success or a humiliation?

Either way, another stay was granted.

* * *

But Ted's good fortune couldn't last forever. Too many people—many of whom in positions of power—wanted Ted dead.

By the winter of 1988, the Florida courts ruled that the question of Ted's competency didn't disqualify him from fulfilling his death sentence. In throwing out the incompetency plea, the reality of Ted's execution looked more and more certain.

He'd die, the papers said, probably early the following year.

This time felt different. I could feel it in my gut. This time it would stick.

\* \* \*

I remember driving one day, either to work or home from it, and I had the radio tuned to KIRO, the local CBS affiliate news station. A story came on about Ted's impending execution, and before I could switch it, the reporter went out to interview people on the streets. I don't know why I kept listening or what I expected to hear—perhaps somber tones as the public remembered Ted's horrible crimes. I braced myself for the familiar sense of second-hand guilt.

Instead, an almost breathless excitement came through the car speakers. Voice after voice sounded ecstatic, barely able to contain the elation that Ted would finally get what he deserved. The whiplash from what I'd expected left me stunned.

After several soundbites of people saying they had no sympathy for his family, especially not his mother, I turned it off.

In the silence, I thought about Louise, one of the most kind, caring people I'd ever known. Over the years, I'd come to further appreciate the sacrifice and courage it took when she, as a young single mother, uprooted her life to move with Ted across the country. I knew she'd stuck by Ted, his most ardent believer. He would always be her golden boy. Could I blame her for standing by him? No. Just as I couldn't blame the mothers of the women Ted had killed for wanting him dead.

But the response from the general public blew me away. Fueled by righteous anger, it seemed they'd lost all grip on their own humanity. It brought to mind certain lessons from my history classes—the bloody gladiatorial games in Ancient Rome, or the crowds that rushed to the Place de la Concorde to witness despised royals get the guillotine during the French Revolution. Somehow it didn't feel like justice; it felt like bloodsport.

As time went on, it only grew worse. People couldn't get enough, and the media was happy to fan the flames. I began to be afraid that some enterprising reporter would finally track us down. Then, once we'd been located, surely others would pile on, like a pack of hyenas chasing down prey.

I couldn't let that happen.

* * *

Around this time, I began to feel like I was losing my mind.

I couldn't sleep. I couldn't eat. I was so distracted at work, I started to fear I'd lose my job.

I became aware of a need, evidently more urgent than food or rest, that I'd never felt before. It was primal. It consumed me completely.

I needed someone to talk to.

After avoiding the topic for the last decade, I couldn't go on any longer without spilling my guts.

Of course, I talked to Don. I've always talked to Don. He'd been there with me through it all, but this exactly described the problem. Don was a part of the drama himself, and he was as exhausted by the whole thing as I was. He, as well as my closest friends, already knew everything forwards and backwards, inside and out. This need of mine demanded new blood.

I can't explain it. All I know is I was completely overwhelmed with the necessity to tell a third party my side of things for the first time. But as this was a monumental risk, it was crucial that whomever I opened up to could understand where I came from. Here I almost lost hope. Who would possibly understand, really understand, unless they'd known Ted, too?

That got my mind going.

I remembered the name of Richard Larsen. He'd known Ted for years. He'd written the book that became the Mark Harmon mini-series, and I still saw his byline regularly in the *Seattle Times*.

My mind kicked into a higher gear. I became certain that, if he was willing to talk to me, he and I would share a common bond. Most people only knew the side of Ted portrayed in the news—the cold-blooded murderer of young women and girls. I didn't know that side. I knew the other Ted. And I suspected that Mr. Larsen did, too.

But one fact threatened to slam the brakes on the entire idea. Richard Larsen was a member of the press—exactly the people I'd been avoiding like the plague. Everyday I prayed that my family wouldn't be found by reporters, so why the hell would I call one voluntarily?

That would be crazy.

* * *

I waited until lunchtime ended. All my colleagues began getting back to work with the revived spirit that comes from a full stomach, and the office hummed with activity.

I knew this would be my best chance. No one was paying attention.

I got up and softly closed the door to my office. This went in violation of my usual open-door policy, but I had to take the risk that it would go unnoticed for a few minutes.

In the quiet of my office, I took a couple deep breaths, hoping that the thousands of cold calls I'd made during my sales career had prepared me for this moment. But I couldn't deny this was different. This was as personal as it got.

Pulling out the Yellow Pages, I found the number for the *Seattle Times* and, with a glance through the window to the rest of the office, I dialed.

I reminded myself that I'd settled on Richard Larsen for a reason. We were, after all, members of the same club: we'd both been deceived by Ted Bundy.

A voice answered, identifying the *Seattle Times* front desk and asking where I'd like my call directed. "Richard Larsen, please."

As soon as I voiced his name, it became real. What did I think I was doing, calling a prominent reporter and author of a bestselling book? What made me think I'd be able to get hold of him?

And if I did, then I'd have to confess my relation to Ted—the very thing I took great pains to conceal—to a total stranger. How would he react?

With relief, I realized I'd most likely get his voicemail. But then, maybe that was worse. How could I say what I had to say on a voicemail? Had I made a huge mistake?

Then it was too late to worry. Richard Larsen answered his phone.

Slipping into sales mode, I introduced myself—my voice didn't even falter when I said Ted's name—and cut to the chase. "I'd like to meet with you."

As I said it, I realized he probably received similar calls all the time from every brand of nutcase. He'd definitely turn me down. If I was him, I'd turn me down.

He didn't turn me down.

He suggested we meet at the 13 Coins by the *Seattle Times* building. "Do you know it?"

I assured him I did. I worked with restaurants all over the city, selling them advertising in our books. I'd become quite familiar with Seattle's prominent eateries, and this was one.

As we made arrangements, I didn't even realize I'd pulled out a pen. When I hung up, I looked down at my appointment calendar. There it read in ink:

*Richard Larsen, 3:30 p.m. Thursday, 13 Coins, Seattle location.*

* * *

13 Coins, located just kitty-corner from the *Seattle Times* building, was a venerable city landmark. With its ceiling-high-backed booths, its hanging model galleon, and its open kitchen showcasing a rolling performance of toques and flames, it never lacked in atmosphere. Due to its proximity to the newspaper's offices, the dining room became a satellite office for hungry reporters, and when I walked in at 3:30 p.m. sharp, I wondered if I'd foolhardily entered the belly of the beast.

The bar glowed with natural light streaming in from the windows. Post lunch but not yet happy hour, the dining room was as quiet as it ever got. As the host greeted me, I scanned for a middle-aged man, and I barely opened my mouth to say I was meeting someone when I caught sight of a gentleman sitting at a two-top table in the far corner, his back to the wall. Instantly I knew him.

Richard Larsen—he quickly told me to call him Dick—looked polished in his suit, but the way he wore it suggested the getup was merely a uniform for his job, which was what he really cared about. A dogged energy surrounded him. His hair looked like it could use a trim.

"You must be Edna," he said, standing to help me with my coat. As he pulled out my chair, I could see a distinct kindness in his eyes. My nerves calmed.

Sitting, I checked the tables surrounding us—all empty—and Dick assured me it wouldn't start getting busy for another hour. He spoke like a man who knew the bar's ebb and flow intimately, and I realized he'd probably done a hundred different interviews in this same room.

I thanked him for seeing me. He brushed it off by gesturing to the beer in front of him, and he asked me what I'd like to drink. I got the attention of a server and ordered a chardonnay.

All this interplay was uniquely charged. We studied one another like cats, nothing falling short of our notice. My time in sales had taught me to read cues, to discern if someone might be open to my spiel. Much was at stake for me personally, and I believe it was the same for him. I'm sure he wondered if I sought to use him, a member of the press, for my own agenda. I had my privacy to uphold; he had his reputation.

Problem was, neither of us had overly aggressive personalities, and we might have stayed in our corners sniffing each other all evening. After a bit of small talk, I bit the bullet. "Can I trust you?" I asked. I told him that I knew he was a reporter with an interest—and an audience— in Ted Bundy. That was both why I hoped to talk to him and what made me concerned to do so. I asked him if what we discussed could remain private, off the record. "I don't want to be in the paper," I said.

Dick looked me straight in the eye. "Edna," he said. "I won't reveal anything we talk about."

I looked back at him. This total stranger. This journalist.

*Trust but don't be deceived*, I thought. Could I trust him? I took a deep breath.

I began talking.

* * *

Over the next hour and a half, I began telling Dick my story, starting back before I'd been born when Ted's mother moved with him across the country from Philadelphia to live with my parents and brother. I told him about Ted's visits to Longbranch and to Arkansas.

We ordered more drinks, and I told him about being a student in Seattle when Ted would drop by, always welcome and adored. Dick told me how he'd admired Ted in those days when he'd been working in politics, seeing in him so much promise.

We swapped stories about how we'd each finally come to terms with the truth. As a reporter, Dick was uniquely positioned to spend one-on-one time with Ted throughout his legal proceedings. In the beginning, he—like the rest of us—couldn't believe Ted was guilty and assumed it was a mistake. As the evidence mounted, eventually Dick couldn't deny Ted's guilt any longer, but he fought that acceptance every step of the way.

"Did you ever suspect?" I asked. "Before?"

Dick shook his head. He told me about a time when he'd visited Ted in Utah, after he'd first been arrested. "He'd gotten rid of his Volkswagen by then," he told me. "He needed to run a few errands, so I lent him my rental."

I almost choked on my wine. "You loaned him a car, after he'd been arrested for attempted kidnapping?"

Dick smiled sheepishly. "Ted was good," he said. "You weren't the only one he had fooled."

Before we left, we arranged to meet up again. "Soon," I said.

Dick had already pulled out his datebook. "How about next week?"

❆ ❆ ❆

At home, I told Don all about our conversation. He'd just gotten home from a jobsite, a hard day of managing his crew. Anna was in her bedroom.

As I spoke, Don stifled a yawn. "I should let you get some rest," I said.

But Don didn't want me to stop. He wanted to hear everything Dick had said. I think that, like me, it did him good to hear that Dick, an objective party to our own trauma, had had a similar experience with Ted. Somehow it validated our journey.

But mostly, I think he could hear in my voice that my burden had somewhat lightened since talking to Dick, and that made him lighter, too.

As we got ready for bed, Don pulled me into a hug. "Just because you're talking to him doesn't mean you can't talk to me, too, you know. Anytime you want to."

"I know," I said, and I did.

\* \* \*

Meanwhile Anna was on a journey of her own, all alone. As the media grew frenzied in their coverage of Ted's impending execution, Anna couldn't have avoided it if she'd tried. And so, at the age of twelve, she began learning—really for the first time—who Ted was and what he'd done.

She described the experience, years later, as shame by proxy. Ted rose up in her mind like a specter, and though she'd never met him, she hated him. She couldn't fathom what kind of monster could have done the things mentioned on TV. And this monster was a part of her family.

But also monstrous was the picture of society she glimpsed, there in the same coverage. People seemingly frothed at the mouth, eager for the chance to send electricity through the veins of another person. She'd never seen that side of society before, and it disgusted her.

Through Ted and then through the public's anticipation of his death, Anna began to learn how dark humanity could be.

She had so many emotions, so many questions, and—God forgive me—nowhere to take them. In fact, I became aware that Anna was trying to protect me. I saw it in the small movements—the way she'd quickly switch off the TV when I entered the room, or her darted glance at my face when his name came up in public. I'd fought her entire life to protect her from the subject of Ted, and now she'd taken the role of protecting me.

And how did I repay her? My own tension made me peevish, snapping at minuscule things around the house. I closed up regarding the very thing she needed to talk about most. I became fixated on keeping her safe.

One memory from around this time period stands out. Anna had been riding her bike in the neighborhood with a friend from school. They'd lost track of the minutes, and when Anna arrived home, she was five minutes late.

Putting her bike away, she walked up to the house from the back yard, and there I was, waiting for her on the back porch with my arms crossed.

There's no way around it—I blew up at her. I flew well and truly off the handle. Anna could only stare back at me, agape. "What?" she managed to mutter, genuinely confused at my reaction to such a small infraction.

After I stormed off, Anna burst into tears, and Don pulled her aside in the quiet of the hallway. She asked him why I'd been, to her mind, so unfair, and he squeezed her with a sad kindness.

"Honey," he said to her. "It's because of Ted."

In that moment, Anna realized she'd never have the luxury of being late, like other kids. She saw then the kind of daughter she needed to be with a mom like me and a family like ours.

* * *

"Do you think it could be genetic?"

Dick and I were at 13 Coins again. As usual, Dick had ordered a beer while I had wine. He'd just taken a sip, which he carefully swallowed before setting down his glass.

He told me there'd been a number of studies about the topic. But it didn't seem to be as easy as genes.

"Well, what do you think?" I told him how my relationship with my own emotions had become electrically charged. Each time I got frustrated, each time I felt my temper slipping, I thought of Ted. "What if whatever's wrong with him is in me, too?"

That was probably the most serious I ever saw Dick. He reached across the table and grabbed my hands. His touch was soft, but his tone was hard as stone. "No," he told me in a way that left no room for argument. "You're not like him. It's not in you."

I knew I'd spend the rest of my life hoping he was right.

* * *

I continued to meet with Dick at 13 Coins. Together we saw the holiday decorations in the dining room go up, twinkling lights that reflected in our glasses, carols overtaking the radio. Against this cheerful backdrop, we continued to talk about Ted.

Dick asked if I'd ever written to him in prison.

I told him about the few times we'd corresponded, including that hurtful exchange in 1986 when I'd asked Ted to confess. I told Dick how, since I'd become a mother myself, I'd begun aching in a whole new way for the families of Ted's victims. In letter after letter, I'd begged him to give up information to help the families. It was the least he could do.

"It didn't work," I said, thinking sourly about his response, the way he'd tried to make me feel guilty for asking. "But I'm sure you knew that."

\* \* \*

Another time I remember we discussed the ethics of the death penalty. Both Dick and I agreed that, in Ted's case at least, he'd be more useful alive.

"Just think what we could learn if we studied him," Dick said. "Maybe enough to stop the next guy before it's too late."

\* \* \*

As much as my meetings with Dick helped—and they did—nothing could take away the constant onslaught of emotional tripwires. I couldn't run a simple errand without seeing Ted's face on magazines in the checkout line, couldn't walk down the street without catching sight of someone reading a newspaper with his name.

At work, I'd become so distracted by it all, so obviously upset, that I couldn't avoid the inevitable any longer. I had to tell my colleagues.

It was lunchtime. As usual, everyone congregated in the conference room, unpacking take-out or pulling open tupperwares from home. As people began to eat, conversation halted, and I knew this was my cue. Nervously, I got everyone's attention.

"You may have noticed that I've been a little...off recently."

Every face smiled back with support, though no one tried to refute my admission.

"There's something I need to tell you—something you deserve to know." I took a deep breath. Would this ever get easier to say? (Not for a long time, but yes.) "Ted Bundy is my cousin."

Total silence followed, a rarity in that office. All around, faces stared at me with what's best described as frank incredulity. These were women who'd heard just about everything, but I'd managed to shock them all.

Then, the dam broke, and the questions started.

I tried to answer them all. I gave an abridged version of Ted's and my relationship and how tough it was for the family. Even with all the questions, I could tell that the core of their curiosity was a concern about me and how I'd been affected. My confession hadn't changed the way they felt about me.

The discussion continued through lunch. But then, as the last bites were eaten and leftovers packed away, the unexpected happened.

Everything went right back to normal.

We all had deadlines and sales to make, books to get to press, and we didn't have time to dwell. We'd become so close over the years that any person's hardship—no matter how mundane or sensational—was absorbed and shared by the group.

We were a team.

I stood and returned to my office, where I got back to work.

* * *

Though the exact date still hadn't been set, everyone expected Ted's execution to take place early in the new year, or spring at the latest. Dick told me that when it happened, he planned to be in Florida. This meant he'd see Ted before the execution and be able to report from there. But it wasn't just for work that he wanted to go. According to him, he had to see it to the end.

I imagined Dick there at the prison with Ted, and I was glad. I knew Louise wouldn't be going, or anyone from the family, and this way he'd have a familiar face by his side. Somehow there was still a part of me that wanted to take care of Ted, to make sure he was okay.

The next time I met with Dick, I could sense he had something on his mind.

"I have a proposition for you," he said.

Curious but wary, I asked him what it was.

"How would you feel about going to Florida?" Dick said he wanted to get my thoughts first, but he was certain the *Times* would agree to pay for it. By that point, they just wanted to do whatever they could to help. "You and Ted were close. Maybe he'd tell you things he hasn't told anyone else, before it's too late."

I understood immediately what he meant. *Bones*, I thought. Dick was suggesting that Ted might give me the locations of the remains of the women they'd never found, maybe even some we didn't know about yet. Authorities still weren't certain how many lives he'd stolen, and his name had been suggested in numerous cold cases.

"Your name will stay out of the paper," he said. "I'll do everything I can to protect you."

I was completely taken aback. *Hell yes*, came my first thought. That ache again flushed over me, the same one that had compelled me to write Ted three years earlier, asking him to confess then. I desperately wanted to help any way that I could. I pictured myself walking into the prison, flanked by police officers. *I can do what everyone else has failed*, I thought. *Because I know Ted*.

But a buzzing in my head got progressively louder as I opened my mouth to answer Dick, and I realized the lie I'd just told to myself.

If I'd learned anything, it was that I didn't really know Ted at all.

The part of me that believed I could make Ted talk was the same part that had believed we'd had a special relationship, the same part that had been manipulated and betrayed by him over and over. Hadn't I learned my lesson? Did I really believe I could get Ted to talk? And what would be the price for my attempt? I remembered, then, the vow I'd made to keep my daughter safe.

I told Dick I'd needed to think about it. He smiled and told me he'd have suggested the same thing.

* * *

As soon as Don returned home that night, I cornered him and told him about the offer. He was really moved by it, proud that Dick had asked. Don's always had the soldier's mindset, seeking out his part to help the community. But even Don had concerns.

That night we sat at the kitchen table and combed through the issue piece by piece. In doing so, Don and I talked in greater depth about our shared trauma than perhaps we ever had. It opened the door, the door I admit I preferred to keep closed, and we learned we were more similar, more aligned than we'd even realized. Call it compatibility. Call it the natural consequence from a shared life. In either case, by the end of the conversation, I knew what I needed to do.

* * *

When I met up with Dick the next time, the holidays were over. Gone were the ribbons and twinkling lights. The soundtrack had traded carols back for soothing background music.

Walking in, I caught a glimpse of Dick seated at the two-top in the far corner, the same table from our first meeting. As I approached, he smiled widely and greeted me with a hug. We sat, and I noticed again the kindness in his eyes. Like our first meeting, I was nervous about what I had to say. I took a breath.

"I can't go to Florida," I said.

I reminded him about the letters I'd written to Ted years earlier asking him to confess when Ted had thoroughly blown me off. I told Dick that I felt Ted kept me as part of his "normal" life, which he clearly worked hard to keep separate from his other life. This separation enabled him to get away with his crimes as long as he did—because on the outside he'd appeared so normal. Keeping up appearances meant a great deal to Ted, and if I was there in Florida, I worried my presence might actually make it harder for him to confess.

That is, if I had any power over him at all, which I suspected I didn't. I once thought we'd had a special relationship. I once thought he'd cared about me. If he did—if that was even possible—then evidently those feelings had never been powerful enough to affect Ted's self-serving actions. He'd do what he felt benefitted him most, period. I was convinced my going to Florida would be fruitless.

And what would be the cost? Up to that point, my family had been able to remain anonymous—the invisibility I desperately needed. If I went to Florida, in spite of Dick's promises, I didn't see how I'd possibly stay a secret. Someone would find out. In my head, I pictured news vans parked outside our house on Beach Drive, journalists showing up at Anna's school. I'd seen the bloodlust of the media. How could I dream of exposing my family to that? They'd come for us, for all of us, and it would change the course of our lives forever.

The last explanation I gave Dick was both the simplest and most personal. I didn't want to see Ted. I didn't want to be in the presence of his evil again. It would be dangerous. He'd duped me, used me, broken my heart, and I was done with him. Sure, shame was part of this—shame I'd been tricked but also shame of being related to him. To face Ted would be to face all that he'd done, and that made me sick.

"Ultimately," I told Dick, "I just want to live a normal life. And not let him dominate it anymore."

When I apologized, he waved it away like a bad smell. He understood, he told me. He'd also worried about the risks, the personal toll, but he felt he had to ask.

When we said goodbye that day, we parted as dear friends. I tried to hide the tears in my eyes as we hugged. That was the last time we met.

Dick continued publishing articles. He easily could have written about me.

He never did.

\* \* \*

In early 2001, I found out that Dick was ill. I wrote to him, telling him how much he meant to me. He wrote back an emotional letter that I've saved to this day. When he died in April of 2001, I cried.

Dick Larsen saved my life. I was lost. He listened to me.

What a gift.

\* \* \*

In mid-January, with only a week's notice, they set the date for Ted's execution. It would occur Tuesday, January 24, 1989.

The public responded as if the holiday season had been extended. I saw reports that said people in Florida planned parties to commemorate the occasion—barbecues, of course—and "Tuesday is Fryday" became a popular slogan. Different bumper stickers cropped up in traffic: some advertised "Bundy Burgers"; others said things like "I'll buckle up when Bundy does."

At her middle school, Anna remembers one morning that week. Leaving the office where she volunteered, she'd taken only a few steps down the carpeted hallway—she can still picture its garish eighties' stripe—when she stopped dead in her tracks.

There in front of her stood a boy wearing a T-shirt printed with the words "Burn, Bundy, Burn." The caption accompanied a cartoon image of Ted in an electric chair. To her, the red ink looked like blood against the white cotton.

Anna froze up. The boy, who was a year or two older, had no clue who Anna was—she'd told only her very best friends about her relation to Ted—but he smirked when he saw her reaction.

Almost instantly, Anna felt a hand on her shoulder. Heidi, one of her closest friends for years, stepped forward and softly guided Anna away.

The rest of the day, she told me decades later, she walked around in a daze.

\* \* \*

Given such short notice, Ted's legal team didn't have much time to get an appeal before the courts. With so many lawmakers in Florida calling for his death, this seems to have been exactly the point.

The following day, top stories around the country reported that Ted was thinking about confessing. The press called it a "bones-for-time" deal, nothing but an attempt at another delay.

But the judge deciding the appeal didn't fall for it. "JUDGE DENIES STAY FOR BUNDY" read the headline in the *Seattle Times* on Thursday, January 19. Let him talk, the Florida courts were saying. But he better do it fast because he only has a few more days left.

During this time, I thought about Ted in his prison cell, though I tried very hard not to. I imagined him looking at calendars, counting down days. I pictured him conferencing with his defense team as they strategized his next move. I wondered if Dick had seen him yet. I wondered if he was sleeping. Don and I were barely sleeping ourselves. Then I wondered if the families of Ted's victims were sleeping. Or if Louise and the Bundys were sleeping.

And then on Saturday, January 21, three days before his execution, Ted began confessing.

\* \* \*

That was hard.

Even if it was what we wanted.

We already knew, of course.

I knew.

I thought of the last day I'd spent with Ted in the U-District, when he'd stood on the street corner, arms out in rapture, proclaiming to the world he was Ted Bundy.

And later when I drove him home, the heater blasted on high, but the air inside the car felt ice cold. I could sense the danger emanating from him. I knew I was in the presence of evil, and it was much, much bigger than me.

I'd glimpsed the other side of Ted that day. I knew he was guilty. So when he finally confessed, it wasn't anything I didn't already know.

But, still.

His confessions went on all weekend.

More than thirty women.

They said later that when he told them their identities, he could barely say their names out loud, choosing instead to write each woman's name on a piece of paper and slide it across the table.

The confessions marked Ted's death to me, in many ways, even more than the day they strapped him to the electric chair.

*  *  *

On Monday evening, the night before the execution, I turned on the news. Anna was in bed, and I had the volume low as I flipped through the channels. In clip after clip, Ted's picture filled the screen along with coverage of various public celebrations. Thousands of people were camped outside the prison gates in Florida, setting off fireworks and breaking intermittently into choruses of "Na Na Hey Hey Kiss Him Goodbye" and chants of "Burn, Bundy, Burn." Much of the crowd appeared to be rather drunk and partying as if it were Super Bowl Sunday. Sick to my stomach, I stood to turn off the TV set when I suddenly recognized Dick's face.

The clip had been recorded earlier. The Starke prison stood in Florida sunshine behind Dick as he reported. He'd been with Ted throughout the day, he said.

Dick looked tired, but otherwise he looked so familiar that I experienced a momentary lapse of space, feeling almost as if we were sitting across a booth, having a private conversation.

Holding a microphone and addressing the camera, Dick reported on Ted's confessions. According to him, Ted knew and accepted that his chance for a delay was over, yet he was still choosing to talk. "Ted is doing this on his own," Dick said with a familiar generosity in his voice.

I sank back into the sofa and wondered if that could be true. An article by Dick had appeared in that morning's *Times*, reporting that Ted, through his emotionally charged confessions, still doled out the details to law enforcement in an obvious tactic for manipulation. He'd give just enough to make them interested, teasing them with what else he might be hiding.

Had something changed Dick's mind since he wrote the article?

I wondered what the chances were that Ted's confessions were now in earnest, as Dick suggested. And if they were, did that mean that Ted had something like a conscience? Was it possible that the Ted I knew and loved hadn't only been a facade?

I became suddenly overcome with memories of Ted as a boy when he'd come to visit the cabin on Longbranch. I could picture him on the shore, stooping to examine the tide pools, showing me hermit crabs—grinning big—before letting them go.

Then I looked again at the screen, and my eyes landed on the hard, white towers in view behind Dick. *Ted's in there*, I thought. I pictured Dick sitting in the room with Ted while he confessed, and a new thought struck.

Ted had a unique gravitational pull about him, his old ability to make a person feel seen. He was a master manipulator. Had Dick, in such close proximity, gotten sucked into Ted's singular orbit, swayed to believe in a side of Ted that he—an old friend—wanted to believe anyway? To Ted, Dick was a member of the press and thus had value. No matter how little time he had left, I was certain Ted would play his game to the bitter end, convinced he'd find a way. His ego would remind him that he'd always managed to come out on top thus far.

Could Ted really be that good, that no one was completely immune, not even Dick? I suddenly became gladder than ever that I'd opted not to go to Florida, to find myself in Ted's orbit.

From where I sat, thousands of miles away, I couldn't believe Ted was trying to save his soul. He was only trying to save his skin.

Though I could be wrong.

I hope I am.

✳ ✳ ✳

The next morning, January 24, I awoke early. In the darkness of the room, my stomach churned. Finally resigning all hope of sleep, I got out of bed and began breakfast.

I turned on the TV, and of course it was all about Ted.

"At 7:16 this morning, Bundy was executed," came the voice of the anchor. The news report showed a drawing of Ted, head shaved, being escorted in chains by prison guards. The anchor said that the guards placed a bag over his head before they strapped him to the electric chair.

"Witnesses report," the anchor continued, "his final words were 'Give my love to my family and friends.'"

In the house, I could hear the rustling sounds of someone else getting up. I feared it might be Anna, so I stood and turned off the TV set before she could see it.

*Ted's high school graduation portrait with an inscription to his grandparents.*

# Christmas Card from Ted to Edna

*Written from prison in 1987.*
*Final correspondence between Ted and Edna.*

*Transcription of entire letter.*

November 22, 1987

Dear Edna and Don,

Much has happened over the years to separate us, but that does not affect the love I have for you.

Have a great Christmas!

Peace

ted

*Lifelong best friends. Left to right: Annie, Margie, Pamela, Edna.*

# True Crime

After the execution, I'd hoped it would all end. I'd hoped the final word had been written, and the world would soon forget, in that fickle way it usually does, all about Ted Bundy.

Instead, as decades have passed, and he endures as an object of fascination—a fixed landmark on our cultural landscape—the secret has remained ours to bear, chafing the wound so it can never quite heal.

I don't take ordinary life for granted. It's a gift to be able to fly under the radar. I look around now at my home full of mementos, and I see evidence of a full life with my family and friends. I see photos of Anna who had a chance to grow up, for the most part, outside of Ted's shadow. I see past decades represented by the hairstyles in snapshots with my girlfriends and art Don and I have collected on our walls. I see seashells from our summer trips to the Oregon Coast and winter trips to Hawaii and Cancun. I see the personal effects of Don and myself as we've grown older. The years have overflowed with laughter, fun, and adventures. Yet, throughout it all, we've worked hard to keep things "normal." I wouldn't have had it any other way.

Still, I'm not sure "normal" is the best way to describe it.

❈ ❈ ❈

One morning about three and a half years ago, Don and I were in the midst of packing up our home to relocate closer to Anna and her family. We looked forward to our upcoming move out of the condominium complex where we lived at that time. It wasn't a bad community, but as is often typical with a homeowner's association, we found residents had the tendency to talk and gossip.

As Don and I packed up the garage, we chatted about all we still had left to do before the move and looked out at the neighborhood, admiring it with the sharpened fondness a person can feel for a place only when they know they're leaving it.

In the front lawn next to our driveway, we saw two figures both with dogs on leashes at their sides, and I recognized our downstairs neighbor and a man I often talked to from the complex. In need of a break, Don and I decided to meander out to say hi. We all greeted one another, and our small group clustered together for that time-old tradition of neighborly chitchat.

I don't remember the topic of our conversation in the beginning, probably some small talk as they asked about our move and where we were going. While we talked, the two dogs wound around, tangling our legs with their leashes, and as I unknotted myself our downstairs neighbor said, "I'm a big true-crime fan."

At that, my inner antenna shot up, all systems on high alert. *Where's this going? What is the threat level?*

"I'm just fascinated with what makes serial killers tick," she went on. When she looked at me, I could tell our neighbor, who had no idea about my family, was urging me to agree.

"Oh, that's interesting," I said, taking care to put a smile on my face. "That's not really one of my favorite genres."

"I really, *really* love Ted Bundy," she said with the fervor of a school girl.

Instantly I felt that familiar electric shock at the mention of his name. I tried to remain composed. "Oh? That's interesting." The smile I'd pasted on began to feel gummy.

But our neighbor must have been unsatisfied with my response, so she turned to address her dog-walking companion. As soon as she did so, I looked at Don and mouthed, *If she only knew!* Don nodded in agreement. *I know!* He made a funny face, and I struggled to suppress a giggle.

But we collected ourselves before anyone noticed, and we carried on with our small talk, eventually excusing ourselves to get back to work.

My mind swam. I couldn't help but think what the gossip mill in that community would have done if they knew who'd been living amongst them.

* * *

Because I don't talk about it, it's been so much easier to keep my connection to Ted private. On only a few rare occasions, in very safe spaces, I've opened up. I've always been extremely cautious.

One of these occasions came about from a remarkable coincidence. For a couple of years, at the urging of some friends, Don and I got involved in building a side business, hoping to add to our revenue stream. As part of the training process, new associates were urged to listen to audio tapes recorded by successful representatives of the venture as they told their stories, meant to inspire and motivate us.

As with most things I commit to, I took my involvement seriously, and I listened to all the tapes, popping them into the cassette deck in my car to play whenever I was driving. Of them all, I remember only one.

At this time, my mother's health began slipping, and it became urgent that I find her a place to live that could provide the care she desperately needed. Although we'd been caring for her at home after my father's death earlier in the year, we couldn't ignore the bald fact that her needs had grown beyond our capabilities. The emotional and physical stress of this time period made me feel like I would die. But I didn't.

One day as I drove to my mother's new adult family home near us, I was so inside my head that I didn't even think about the tape currently playing in my cassette deck. Without knowing it, I began to tune into the voice sounding over my speakers.

The man on the tape told his story in heartbreaking detail of how his oldest son had been diagnosed with cancer. Then, despite everything the doctors could do, the child had died. Through the pain, somehow, he and his wife found the strength to keep going.

I vividly remember sitting in my Ford Explorer in my mother's driveway, listening to the end of the tape, openly sobbing. The man's story stayed with me much longer than my time with that particular business venture.

Not long afterwards, I started a new job as an independent insurance agent at a brokerage firm in Bellevue, selling long-term care insurance. On my first day I was introduced to their top producing agent, who was only too happy to share his knowledge with me and agreed to let me listen in on his calls.

I immediately recognized his name and, more importantly, his voice.

By the look on my face, he could tell something was up, so I blurted out, "I heard your tape." I told him how much it had meant to me. Very quickly, we became friends.

I learned that he was still very successful with the side business while also being a top broker in long-term-care insurance. I really admired him, but as we got closer, I felt as if our dynamic was a little uneven since I knew so much about his past trauma from the outset. The lopsided notion came entirely from me. He never pried into my personal life. He never asked leading questions about me. But one day, as we were sharing stories about how complicated families can be, my heart began pounding. I knew I wanted to tell him my secret. I knew he was a safe place.

"Oh, yeah," I began, nervous but resolute. "I've had some difficult things in my family, too."

Then I told him.

I could see his posture change as he bore the weight of the information. "Oh, my God," he said. He asked a few questions, and we related over some similar parts of our journeys.

After that day, he never brought it up again, always careful to follow my lead. I appreciated that. The friendship we'd begun only deepened, and he and his wife have remained friends of Don's and mine for over fifteen years.

Our dynamic wasn't lopsided anymore.

\* \* \*

It's a funny thing, the human desire to even out a relationship this way. Most of the time I find myself on the other end of the imbalance. For those who know who I am, they feel comfortable confiding in me their darkest troubles. I've learned that everyone carries burdens. My relation to Ted gives them permission to open up to me.

This is an aspect I don't mind.

\* \* \*

Even though it all happened so long ago now, the story still follows us, and new angles continue to come to light.

One recent afternoon, Don and I met for lunch at Harbor Lights in Tacoma with a number of old friends from his high school and college days. Eight of us sat around the table and reminisced, shooting the breeze as old friends do. Though always included in the conversation, I was the sole outlier of the group, the only one who didn't attend either Bellarmine Prep or Stadium High School. So I was a little surprised when Michael, the school friend of Don's seated across from me, asked me how my brother was doing.

Gratified that he'd remembered my family, I told Michael that John was doing well, and I thanked him for asking.

"I really liked your brother," Michael said.

Michael retired as a public defender in Tacoma, though he'd started his career as a Pierce County deputy prosecutor. I didn't remember Michael and John ever crossing paths, so I asked him how they knew one another.

"John came to me to ask for advice on something," Michael said. "During the Ted Bundy thing."

Instantly Don's eyes and mine found each other. "Oh, yeah?" I said, urging Michael for further details.

From there, Michael launched into his own brush with the Ted story, one which, until then, I'd only known pieces.

* * *

When the police in Seattle began closing in on Ted as a suspect, they contacted all of us in his family. In an initial interview, John had told Detective Robert Keppel that he and Ted had enjoyed hiking together in the early 1970s after John moved back to Seattle. They'd taken turns choosing the routes. If Ted led last time, John would spearhead the next hike, and vice versa.

Later, police again contacted John and asked him to show them the areas where Ted had led them on their hikes.

This was in October of 1975, back when we all still believed Ted's arrest had been a mistake, and John's priority lay in supporting his cousin. By then John, like Don, had learned things that led him to worry Ted might have been guilty of smaller crimes—theft, voyeurism—but definitely not murder. He worried that in the detective's pursuit to build a murder case, they'd be inclined to skew innocent details or coincidences, and he didn't want to be a part of that. Ted's own attorney advised John that he had already cooperated sufficiently with the detectives, and he shouldn't agree to the hike.

But John didn't want to be uncooperative with the police nor impede their investigation. Torn about how to proceed, and with me still unreachable in Alaska, John related his situation to Don.

Don told John he had an old friend now working as a deputy prosecutor for Pierce County, and he suggested it might be a good idea to ask his advice. Then Don put John in contact with Michael.

When John met up with Michael, John asked him what he thought he should do. Since he didn't believe Ted was actually guilty of murder, should he agree to go on the hikes with Detective Keppel even though Ted's attorney had advised him against it?

"Well," Michael said to John, "have you done anything wrong?"

John assured him he hadn't.

"Then cooperate," Michael said simply. Despite John's allegiance to his cousin and reservations in the police's case, Michael advised John to take the detectives where he'd hiked with Ted. "It'll either exonerate him or incriminate him," he said. But either way, it was John's responsibility to help the police.

Days later, Detective Keppel showed up at the law firm where John worked with a subpoena. John told me later he welcomed the subpoena, because as he still felt conflicted about the hike, at least a subpoena insured he'd be following legal advice and that he'd get paid for the day.

Unfortunately, John wasn't allowed to go home to change his clothes first, so he went hiking with the Seattle homicide detective that day in his suit and loafers.

❊ ❊ ❊

John remembered the places Ted wanted to explore, because he thought they were boring. When it was John's turn to choose a route, he'd pick trails that took them to beautiful Alpine meadows with views of Mount Rainier, places that were particularly scenic. Ted's hikes often trailed along power lines and the edges of housing developments or by old farms and barns. But he led the detective to the places as asked, all the while sweating in his suit, feet blistering inside his loafers.

After he finished the hike, Detective Keppel never mentioned it to John again, and he was left to assume the day had been a waste of every-one's time.

\* \* \*

In the waterfront dining room of Harbor Lights, before the subject could change, Michael asked if John ever learned the significance of those hikes. Due to Michael's position in the prosecutor's office, he'd been privy to information not shared with us at the time, and he recalled that the day hadn't been the waste of time John had assumed.

It turns out John's hikes took the detective right near both of Ted's major "dump sites," in mountainous regions off I-90 and Highway 18 in the foothills of the Cascades. It was in those areas where police had recovered remains from Lynda Ann Healy, Susan Elaine Rancourt, Roberta Kathleen Parks, Brenda Carol Ball, Denise Marie Naslund, and Janice Ann Ott, as well as others still unidentified. Those hikes with John had substantiated Ted's familiarity with the area.

It seems likely Ted had been using his hikes with my brother to scout out potential places to leave the bodies of his victims.

It wasn't until after our recent lunch with Don's old school friends that we began putting these pieces together.

\* \* \*

Not long ago, I had a phone call from my friend Jeanie, the one who gamely drove across the country with me in the Opel back in 1972. We'd only seen one another a few times since then, both of us busy students then young mothers with thousands of miles between us, and after all the news came out about Ted, I'd never reached out to her to talk about it, so hunkered down in my own survival. I wasn't sure what—if anything—Jeanie even knew.

Comfortably, Jeanie and I spoke about old times and caught up on one another's lives. I learned that Jeanie, now retired, had taught psychology for years as a professor at a college in Missouri. As she'd neared retirement, she said, she began ending her class with a personal anecdote.

Before releasing them from the final lecture, she told her students that she'd once had dinner with the infamous serial killer, Ted Bundy.

I was momentarily shocked. "I wasn't sure what you knew or remembered," I said.

Jeanie told me she'd immediately realized who Ted was as soon as she saw him in the news, remembering the word games we'd all played in the park and our dinner at Liz's house. She told me she'd wanted to reach out to me, but then she put herself in my shoes. She knew what a nightmare it had to be for our family and rightly assumed I'd be sensitive talking about it. "I didn't want to impose," she said.

I was incredibly touched.

According to Jeanie, when she told her students about her dinner with Ted, it never failed to get their attention. She related to them that she never would have guessed the man she met and shared a meal with could have been capable of such horrific acts. Even with her interest in psychology, even though she considered herself a good judge of character, she warned her students that she'd never intuited any red flags or bad feelings about Ted.

"It's a good lesson," she said to me. Many of her students were studying criminology, and she wanted them to understand that they couldn't always rely on their gut feelings. Sometimes our gut feelings are wrong.

Greatly moved, I thanked her for telling me. I like to think this personal anecdote of Jeanie's, offered to students who'd go on to work in various jobs and fields, has somehow stolen something from Ted's terrible crimes to infuse a little good back into the world.

\* \* \*

It's strange, living in a house with Ted's letters.

I don't think about them as much these days, but for years I felt as if they were sort of alive. I'd sense their essence, even inside their box, sealed tight, tucked inside the cabinet. They felt dangerous. I had to keep them safe, or more accurately, to keep everyone else safe from them.

It's not the words in the letters that have this effect on me. It's knowing who wrote them. They came from Ted's mind, from his hand.

But I could never throw them away. If I were to let them out of my care, I couldn't be certain where they'd end up, what other hands might find them. I don't even like to touch them myself, preferring to wear white gloves whenever I handle them. I don't want any of Ted to rub off.

But there's more to it than this. I realized, even at the time we were corresponding, that whether I liked it or not, Ted's letters were a part of history. Having majored in the subject in college, history is something I greatly respect. With a value for historical documentation in mind, I've often wondered if Ted understood the consequences of his decision to angrily return my letters back to me, as it gave me both sides of our exchange. Even though I never planned to show them to anyone, I've safeguarded the letters for decades.

But it's an uncomfortable stewardship.

\* \* \*

Not long ago, I decided to make copies of Ted's letters. I needed hard copies that I could hold in my hands, unlike the real letters, which, as I've said, I only like to handle with gloves.

For some reason, one letter Ted wrote to my parents is legal-sized, 8.5 by 14 inches. I have no idea why, perhaps that was the only paper he could get in prison that day. All I know is that—as I went about making copies of all Ted's letters—this one proved too large for my home office equipment. With some trepidation, I realized this meant I needed to shepherd it out of the house and into the world.

I took it to a UPS Store.

At the counter, the clerk pointed me toward the copier and gave me an access code, then she asked me if I needed assistance.

"No!" I said with more insistence than I intended. "No, I can do it." In and out without drawing attention to what I was copying—this was my plan.

After I'd made certain the helpful clerk didn't follow me to the machine, I retrieved the letter and lined up the first page on the glass, then I got into the settings menu on the copier to switch it to the larger legal-size. I could feel the clerk watching me as I did this, ready to rush to my aid. I had to work fast.

Satisfied that I'd done it, I pressed the button, and the machine came to life, scanning Ted's handwriting, making a double. It brought to mind the process of mitosis—one cell splitting and becoming two.

But when the machine spit out the copy, I immediately saw that it was impossible to read, the original too light. So back into the settings menu I went, looking for a way to crank up the contrast.

"Is there a problem?"

I spun around. The clerk had come over, and her hand reached for the copy on the tray to see what was wrong. I snatched it up fast.

"I just need to heighten the contrast," I told her. She watched over my shoulder as I did so to see that it was done right. I patiently waited until she'd returned to her station at the counter before proceeding.

Alone again, I pushed the button. This time it worked.

As I went through and made copies of the rest, I watched business as usual go on in the store, customers coming in and out, running inane errands in their daily life. I saw myself through their eyes, just some lady at the copier. *If only they knew what I'm copying*, I thought, and I admit, I felt a very small sense of pleasure in the secret. An inside joke with myself.

Even still, when I left, I can't count how many times I checked the glass to be certain I hadn't left any pages behind.

\* \* \*

A few years ago, anticipating the thirtieth anniversary of Ted's execution, a new wave of public interest hit. Anna saw it coming before I did. She's always more tuned in to popular culture, especially in regards to the family, knowing which movie star has been cast to play Ted in whatever new dramatization they're making. She called up her father and warned Don that we would start seeing his name all over the place again. "You have to prepare Mom."

But nothing could have prepared me for the email I received sometime during that period from a producer at a TV production company in England. Though very professional, she wanted to know if she could ask me some questions about my cousin Ted. She offered to travel to my home or even fly me to London for the interview, all expenses to be compensated. Almost fifty years after he'd become an object of public interest, I'd finally been discovered by the press.

I remember the feeling of shock. *How the hell did they find me?* I still don't know for sure.

Thankfully it was an email, so I didn't have to respond immediately. Still, it represented a possible threat to our anonymity, and I felt a desire to get it managed as quickly as possible, worried she might call or—God forbid—show up at my door if they didn't get a response. I didn't know what to expect.

The producer wanted to know if I'd be interested to finally tell "my story." My stomach churned at the thought. My story was exactly the thing I'd been hiding most of my life. Why would I want to willingly release it to the world?

Quickly I let Don and Anna know about the email, and it shook them up, too. Anna even wanted to consult with an attorney friend to make sure we were protected, and he advised her to have me shut it down or risk losing control.

That gave me my response. Only a few hours had passed, but it felt much longer.

"I consulted with my family and an attorney," I wrote back, something to that effect, "and we decided that we'd prefer to stay anonymous."

Gratefully, the producer respected my wishes and never pursued anything further.

Still, in spite of the worry, in spite of the threat to the quiet, normal life I value so dearly, an idea had been planted. Somewhere deep in my subconscious, something began to awaken.

*Edna and Don*

# Jury Duty

Don tells a story of when he got called in for jury duty.

This was in the early-to-mid-nineties. We still lived in West Seattle, and the summons came at a particularly bad time, though I guess it always does. Don had been working relentlessly. His back was killing him, and he needed a break. But breaks were hard to take since he worked for himself and didn't get paid for days off. Jury duty would not only force Don out of his paycheck but rob him of the rest he needed for his back.

He knew I was worried about his health, but he assured me it would be okay. This was his duty, he said, just like going into the Marine Corps had been. Don believes the number one job in society has always been the soldier. Without the soldier, he says, no society can exist. Without order, we have chaos.

And anyway, he reminded me, a summons didn't mean he'd actually serve on a jury. His plan was to show up for the required days, stay off the radar, and never be assigned to a trial. Then he could consider his civic duty fulfilled and get back to work.

"Or take a break," I reminded him, but I don't remember getting a response.

* * *

Arriving at the courthouse on the morning he was due to report, Don found himself in a security line to get into the building. He checked his watch and scanned the line to calculate how fast he could reasonably expect it to go. This is the way Don's mind works. He's always running the numbers, doing the math. As he scanned, his eye caught onto a man close to the front. There was a tightness in the guy's shoulders, a clenched posture that Don knew he recognized.

Then the memory struck.

Don had built a house for him a few years earlier. The guy worked for the post office, Don said, but what he really wanted was to be a cop. To this end, he'd volunteered with the police, sometimes getting asked to help out with things like crowd control or a neighborhood watch. Most importantly to the guy, this qualified him to wear an auxiliary badge and carry a gun.

He'd worn the shoulder holster to meetings with Don, meetings merely to talk about the construction job. It makes it really hard to have a conversation, Don said, when the other guy's wearing a gun.

"Do you always wear the shoulder holster?" Don had asked him finally.

"No," the guy said.

"Well, why are you wearing one now?"

He didn't have a good answer.

But he had to stop wearing it when the police got rid of him and took away his badge. Don learned later that the guy had gone into a convenience store, flashing the auxiliary badge, and he'd roughed someone up. When Don met the guy's wife while working on their house, he thought there was a good chance the guy was roughing her up, too.

Up ahead in the security line, the guy emptied his pockets into a tray before stepping through a metal detector. Don watched, wishing the machine was a son-of-a-bitch detector.

It wasn't, and the machine didn't beep. The man was given back his effects and welcomed into the hall of justice.

*  *  *

Once upstairs, Don checked in with the bailiff, who gave him a questionnaire to complete and gestured for him to take a seat. The chairs, Don noted, were the hard plastic ones that didn't do anyone's back a favor.

He made sure to sit far away from the guy he'd recognized downstairs. Taking out the form, Don uncapped his pen, eyes already scanning.

*Describe any ethical reasons that may prevent you from serving as a juror.*

When Don tells this part of the story, he laughs. *Does 'I have better things to do' count?* he thought. But he left the section blank.

*Have you or a person with whom you have a significant relationship ever worked in law enforcement?*

*Have you or a person with whom you have a significant relationship ever been a victim of a crime?*

He understood that they were trying to get an idea how he felt about the police.

*What is your general belief regarding the death penalty?*

This topic stirs a lot of thoughts for Don—and for all of us. Instantly memories of *Burn, Bundy, Burn* ran through his mind, as he remembered how difficult it had been to come to terms with the execution of a family member.

He marked *Strongly Opposed* and moved on.

*Has anyone with whom you have a significant relationship ever been charged with a capital crime?*

Ever a numbers guy, he wondered, statistically, how many people answered *yes* to that one.

As he put pen to paper, Don said that's when he got the feeling it would come for him, the storm we spent our lives outrunning. It would flood the building, an inch in the basement to start, but the water would rise up to find him. He just hoped he'd be gone before it could.

*Yes*, Don answered, and he left it at that.

※ ※ ※

After he turned in his form, the rest of the day was spent trying to find a comfortable way to sit in his chair as Don read from his book, a Dick Francis mystery. He'd made sure to bring something light with enough plot to pass the time.

At one point late in the afternoon, someone appeared and called out names to go to a neighboring courtroom for jury selection. A hearing had just been confirmed. Fortunately, Don's name wasn't called.

It wasn't until later that he looked around and realized his old friend, the guy with the shoulder holster, was gone. His must have been one of the names called.

*Better him than me*, Don thought, though I think even then he wondered if that was true.

\* \* \*

On day two, Don finished his book.

After lunch, he got to chatting with a pair of friendly young women. They really hoped to get put on a jury, they told him. They thought it sounded glamorous and important. "Maybe we'll all get chosen together," said one woman. "And it's one of those trials that gets in the papers and goes on for weeks."

"You should be the jury foreman," added the second woman, enthusiastically.

Don just smiled politely. It felt wrong to admit to them he wanted nothing less.

While they talked, Don grew aware of a tall, skinny man sidling into his row to sit in the chair right next to his, despite the fact that there were many empty seats. The sound of their conversation must have brought him over, since it quickly became apparent that the man was keen to talk.

He directed his chatter mostly at Don, and his topics came in an unrelated stream, from World War II to the size of Don's shoes. Don quickly discerned that there was something slightly loose about him. A screw that hadn't been properly tightened.

When the man took a breath, Don sensed he'd been working himself up to the topic he really wanted to discuss. *Oh, boy*, Don thought. *Here we go.*

"Hey, you know, have you heard about those colonies on Mars?"

I've known Don a long time, and these are moments he can't resist. I'm sure the boredom of the past couple days didn't help. So, it came as no surprise to me to hear that Don answered, without even pausing,

"Yeah."

The tall man was so thrown by Don's answer, he almost lost his train of thought. "You do!?"

By this point, Don said, he thought the man had to be messing with him. He expected the next thing to come from his mouth to be a confession.

That wasn't to be. "It must take a lot of equipment to build a colony on Mars," the man said.

Don agreed that it would. The women he'd been conversing with were clearly listening, and they threw Don glances to see if he could be serious. Don's eyes twinkled, savoring the absurdity.

"But I have a question," the man said.

*Only one?* Don thought.

"How do you suppose they got all that equipment up there?" the tall man asked.

Don couldn't resist another yank of the chain. "You know," he said.

"No, what?"

With authority, Don answered, "Teleportation."

At this, the women had to forcibly restrain themselves from laughing, but somehow they managed.

The tall man's eyes widened. "Do you think so?"

Don kept his tone serious. "Think about it. It's the only way."

The tall man nodded, taking this in. "Have you been there?" he asked.

"No," Don said, thinking fast. "But I'm going in six weeks. My, uh, brother's there." That seemed appropriate. Sometimes Don wished his brother was on another planet.

"Wow," the tall man said, impressed. "What are you going to do up there?"

"Well, I'm a builder," Don decided a little truth would help his plausibility. "So they need people like me."

The tall man nodded as if it made all the sense in the world.

The man had a lot more questions, and Don worried he wouldn't be able to keep up the ruse. To his neighbor's disappointment, he excused himself to find a bathroom.

*How weird was that?* Don thought as he stepped into the hallway. At least it had provided some entertainment for a few minutes. He was already thinking about how he'd tell me the story later.

When he returned, Don found a place to sit on the opposite side of the room, but he needn't have bothered. They were soon dismissed and asked to return in the morning.

\* \* \*

On the third day, Don's name got called.

Walking out with the others, he recognized the two women he'd enjoyed talking to the day before, still behind in their seats. When they saw he'd been called, they waved excitedly.

Despite his resolve to make it through jury service without actually serving on a jury, Don says he felt something like excitement as he followed the others to a nearby courtroom for jury selection. "Not a bad tactic," Don said to me later. "Put anyone into a state of boredom, and most people will be falling over themselves to do just about anything."

As they were ushered towards the benches, he noticed the tall, skinny man with an interest in Mars taking a seat near the front. Thankfully there were still lots of open benches. Determined to stay off the radar, Don found a mostly empty row and settled in.

Almost as soon as he'd sat, they were all asked to stand again, and the door to the courtroom opened.

A judge entered, followed by a small group of lawyers in suits, the younger ones carrying bankers' boxes or rolling in plastic filing cabinets. Don was struck by the sudden gravity in the room. This implicit respect for authority. It reminded him of the military.

Once the judge and attorneys settled in, they were all seated again, and that's when Don noticed that one of the figures who'd entered with the lawyers didn't quite fit in.

The boy—that's the way Don described him to me later—looked very young and moved stiffly inside his suit. While the others arranged folders and poured glasses of water, he merely sat staring forward in his chair.

"Wonder what he did," he heard someone nearby whisper, craning their neck to try to get a better look.

*Allegedly*, Don thought.

* * *

Over the course of the day, they whittled the jury pool down to eighteen members. Don remained, along with his talkative neighbor, the Mars man.

Those remaining were asked to file into the jury box at the front of the courtroom. As they moved camp, Don noticed one of their ranks slip away and approach the bench. In Don's earshot, the man complained to the judge about having been dragged downtown for jury duty. He'd moved to the U.S. a couple years previously, and he didn't feel he should have to do it.

While he had the judge's ear, another grievance popped up. He'd been given a traffic ticket earlier that month after being caught on camera speeding in a school zone. He didn't find that fair, either, and apparently, he wanted the judge to dismiss both offenses. "This is no way to welcome people into your country, Your Honor."

The judge didn't appear moved. She asked him to take his seat in the jury box.

\* \* \*

The defense attorney—Don learned he was a public defender assigned to the case—made a presentation to the jury. As he spoke, Don couldn't help but watch the young man. He sat silently, not reacting, as his lawyer talked about him like he wasn't even there. Don couldn't help but feel bad for him.

The attorney explained that his client, who'd recently turned twenty-four, had been in juvenile detention since he was a teenager and then incarcerated as an adult, but he'd served his maximum sentence and was due to be released. The prosecution didn't want that, predicting a propensity to reoffend. "Considering his history, most people already assume he's guilty. Could you be open to the idea that my client is not guilty of everything he's been accused of?"

The attorney was looking right at Don, who realized the question wasn't rhetorical. "I don't know if he's guilty of anything. I don't know him at all." *Or care to,* Don thought. "I haven't heard the case, so until proven otherwise, I'm going to assume he's innocent."

From his seat on the other side of the courtroom, Don saw the lead prosecutor turn and clock his face. He made a note on the legal pad in front of him.

\* \* \*

After the defense had finished, the lead prosecutor slid from his chair and stood in front of the potential jurors. Immediately he launched into a detailed explanation of what had put the defendant into the system in the first place. As a teen, he had been charged with sexually assaulting and raping scores of women and children, ages four to eighty-two. The later ones were particularly bad, the prosecutor said, as he'd graduated to knifepoint. While incarcerated as a young adult, during an evaluation he'd been asked to draw pictures of whatever he wanted. He chose to draw violent pictures, showing children, girls, and women being cut up into pieces. "This isn't someone we want back on the streets," said the prosecutor.

Don could feel the bile rising in his throat. He looked at the young man again, up and down. Don wondered about his family. Were they the ones who'd bought him the suit for court? Would they be at the trial?

Without meaning to, Don thought about his journey coming to believe in Ted's guilt. The biases he'd had to fight, the blinders he'd had to learn to take off his eyes to see the facts for what they were. He had experience doing that. Not a lot of people did.

* * *

When the lead prosecutor again took his seat, the bailiff brought over a stack of papers for the judge. She flipped through them for a moment before asking everyone to leave the room while they took care of some business.

As Don filed out of the pews, a sinking feeling fell over him. He had a pretty good idea that the stack of papers were the questionnaires they'd submitted on their first day. *They're going to want to talk to me*, he thought. He'd nearly forgotten about the storm he'd sensed coming for him ever since he'd filled in his answers. It hadn't forgotten about him.

Out in the hall, he said he felt like a school kid waiting to see the principal. Every time he heard a door open, he looked up, waiting for his time.

Soon the bailiff appeared from the doorway and, sure enough, he called out Don's name.

When he returned to the courtroom, any earlier excitement he'd sensed had completely disappeared. Approaching the bench, he couldn't help but feel he was the one on trial. On both sides, the attorneys studied Don, poised to determine whether they'd choose to keep him as a juror or exercise their right to eliminate him.

The judge greeted him and thanked him for coming to talk to them. Don tried to make a joke to cut the tension. Unusual for him, it didn't work. From this angle, he could see the stack of papers, and sure enough, they were the questionnaires. One had been pulled from the others, and it sat in front of the judge. Don recognized his own handwriting.

The judge explained that, before they moved forward with the jury selection, they had a few questions they'd like to hear more about. Don nodded, his throat too dry to speak.

"How do you feel about the police?"

Choosing his words carefully, he explained that he'd been in the military, and he believed in law and order. He supported the police, he said, so long as they were working to achieve it.

From the corner of his eye, he saw the lead prosecutor mark another note on his legal pad.

The judge looked again at Don's form. "You wrote that you don't believe in capital punishment."

Don wondered if those old city buildings had air conditioning. It suddenly felt very hot. "I've been around long enough," he said, "to see that it mostly applies to poor people and people of color."

Another note went onto the prosecutor's legal pad. Meanwhile Don almost thought he caught a smile cross the judge's face, though it might have been only a shadow.

"I see from your form," she went on, and then Don knew it was coming, "that you know someone who's been charged with a capital crime."

Don nodded, hoping he wouldn't have to get into specifics.

"And would it be okay if I ask, what was the resolution of that case?"

The tension was playing tricks on Don, and he was surprised to find he felt emotional. He had to hold it together.

"He was found guilty by a jury."

"And what kind of sentence did he receive?"

"Capital punishment," Don replied.

"And may I ask, what happened after that?"

"He was executed."

The air left the room, like the moment after lightning strikes. Don could feel every single pair of eyes find him, including those of the young defendant who, up until that point, had been mostly staring at the table in front of him.

The judge looked shocked. When she spoke again, her voice had developed a soothing quality, like honey or a favorite old sweater. She asked Don if he believed, with an event like that in his past, that he'd be able to put any personal history aside and hear the case fairly, for what it was.

"Yes," Don answered.

He was surprised to notice that, at some point without his knowing, his mind had changed, and now he very much wanted to be on the jury. *I could do this,* Don thought. Far from making him biased, he was convinced his personal experience would actually help him see both sides and judge fairly. *Edna will understand. I'd be the best goddamn juror they could ask for.*

But the judge wanted to push the point. Though this wasn't a capital murder case, she wanted to know if Don felt he'd be able to vote for the death penalty in a case if he felt the law proved it was required.

"If that's what the law proved," Don said, "I would vote for the law."

Don didn't mistake it this time—she smiled. As she picked up his questionnaire to put it back in the stack with the rest, almost as an after-thought, she said, "If you don't mind me asking, who was it that was executed?"

There it was. The storm had found him at last. It was as if the door burst open, and a wave of dark water gushed inside, flooding the courtroom.

Don's heart pounded. He hated to have to say the name, to make that connection. He hated to have to conjure all that my cousin had done, all the families he'd destroyed. We'd been trying so hard for years to leave it behind, yet still it haunted us. He haunted us.

"Ted Bundy," he said.

Later when he told me the story, he said that their jaws actually dropped.

On his legal pad, the lead prosecutor made another mark.

\* \* \*

The judge had more questions after that. This always seems to be the case, once Ted's name is dropped.

They kept Don in the room for probably another ten minutes. The judge politely led Don through a new series of questions, which he answered as best he could, though he admitted to me later he was fighting his emotions the whole time. She was nothing but respectful, merely wanting to know more about his relationship with Ted, more about my relationship with Ted, and what our interactions had been like with the investigators. But Don had done enough talking about Ted to last a lifetime.

Everyone in their small group hung onto his every word, literally perching on the edges of their seats to hear. Don saw the defendant look him up and down—the same once-over Don had done on him earlier—as if seeing him in a new light. What that light was, Don couldn't say.

After the questions were over, Don's brow dripped with sweat. The judge called to the bailiff to escort Don back out with the rest of the jury pool. But before he left, she turned again to Don and very kindly thanked him for sharing the information.

Don, who was still choked up, could only nod.

＊ ＊ ＊

Back in the hall with the others, Don found a seat. In his head, he did what he always does—he ran the numbers. What were his chances of serving on the jury now, due to nothing else but his relationship to Ted?

He hoped they'd be able to see past it. He hoped they'd see that it could actually help make him a great juror.

＊ ＊ ＊

On day four, Don was told he'd been dismissed from his jury service by the prosecution. He was never given a reason why.

As he left, the man with the traffic ticket glared at him resentfully while his talkative friend, the Mars man, slid over to take his seat in the jury box.

*Anna with her uncle, John.*

# Trivia Night

When Anna transferred to the University of Washington—becoming a Husky just like I'd been, and just like Ted—she took a course in Abnormal Psychology. At the time, she had thoughts that maybe she'd go on to law school and become a criminal prosecutor. While taking the course, she couldn't help but think about Ted.

She didn't know then just how fitting this was since Ted had studied Psychology at the very same school, likely in the very same buildings and classrooms.

Out of the house and away from my protective wing, Anna thought how little she knew about Ted, and she thought that maybe she should know. Perhaps it was an important part of who she was.

Of course, she didn't tell me any of this at the time. She told me later, not long ago. We talk so much now.

She said that one day after her classes, she had some research to do for a paper in another course, something that required looking through old archives of the *Seattle Times*. She remembers going to Suzzallo Library that late afternoon, a Gothic brick building that—with its vaulted ceilings and grand staircase—suggests in another life it might have been a medieval cathedral or brooding manor on a windswept moor. There's a reason it's probably the most recognizable building on campus. The place oozes with atmosphere.

It was perhaps this atmosphere that helped put the idea in Anna's mind. After getting a librarian to help her with the microfiche machine, which was cumbersome and difficult to load, Anna quickly got the hang of it. She found she could change the rolls herself as well as the librarian had, and she made it through all of her research faster than she'd expected.

That was when the thought struck. Why not just go back into the archives a little farther? She knew the years to try—starting in 1974. She could read what really happened. She could finally look the damned thing in the face.

Checking both ways, as if reading old newspaper articles was against the law, Anna loaded the film into the machine.

*Yep, there it is,* came her sinking thought as an article appeared on the screen, the manifestation of a truth she'd never been allowed to see.

The headlines alone were disturbing enough, but other words kept jumping out, words that had become recently familiar—street names, buildings, bars not far from where she sat at that moment. Much of what she read had taken place in that very neighborhood, Seattle's University District, to women who were students just like her.

Anna says she felt sick. Her heart raced. As she read, the words ate at her like poison. *This is really bad,* she remembers thinking.

After a few articles, Anna finally had to shut down the machine. She didn't feel any better off for what she'd learned. She certainly didn't feel as if it had taught her something about herself.

\* \* \*

It was in that Abnormal Psych class that Anna tried to tell her study lab about her relation to Ted. They were a small group, and the setting seemed about as appropriate as it would ever get. If she said it casually, she thought, maybe it wouldn't feel so heavy.

Instead, she was met with appalled stares and lots of questions. Only about six or seven years had passed since Ted's execution, and her classmates still remembered.

Anna recalls feeling as if she owed them answers to their questions, as if her relation to Ted obligated her with this responsibility, so she let them ask her anything they wanted, and she tried her best to satisfy them.

Anna didn't like the way her disclosure left her open and exposed. She felt laid bare, exhausted.

\* \* \*

After that, she became more choosy. She didn't guard it quite as protectively as I did, one generation removed, but still she preferred to keep it to herself.

Whenever she'd start dating new people, she'd use it as a barometer to gauge their reactions. The worst, she said, was when it made them treat her differently.

She tended to gravitate towards men who took the family secret in stride, as if the whole thing didn't really concern Anna, as if they didn't find the fact of her relation to Ted that big of a deal.

All she really wanted—all any of us really wanted—was to be normal.

* * *

A few years ago, Anna went down to a local coffee shop on the island in Puget Sound where she lives. It's the kind of place that's still unknown to tourists, where locals congregate and those behind the counter already know everyone's drink orders. On Wednesday nights, the coffee shop sort of fuses with the bar next door to host Trivia Night, which always packs the tables.

This particular Wednesday was a summer night, our magical season in the Pacific Northwest with clear skies and that soft sunlight that glimmers well into the evening. Anna could hear the trivia just beginning when she arrived, but she spotted some friends seated at an outdoor table and signaled to them. Forget trivia, she decided. These evenings were best spent outside, sipping wine under the sky and catching up with friends.

Having secured her drink order, Anna emerged again moments later and snaked her way around the other crowded tables in the seating area, crammed with locals also keen to take advantage of the nice evening. As she shimmied through the crowd toward her party, one of Anna's friends at the table spotted her and yelled, loud enough for everyone to hear, "Oh, my God, Anna, you never told me you're Jeffrey Dahmer's cousin!"

Every single head swiveled to look at Anna. The relaxing summer evening she'd envisioned disintegrated. She wanted to curl up and die.

Instead, she waved, acknowledging her audience, aware that she knew a good number of people in the crowd. The island suddenly felt very small.

"Nope," she said, a pained smile on her face for the sake of the crowd, "not Dahmer. The other one."

Her friend smacked her husband, seated next to her, in the chest. "You told me it was Dahmer!"

Her husband rubbed his chest. "I knew it was one of them."

Meanwhile, Anna had finally made it to the table and sat down, though reaching her destination did nothing to deter people from staring. She recognized the hungry look on their faces. She'd seen it before.

She pulled her chair in tighter.

Anna described the next part as if someone had snapped their fingers. Just like that, her friend—the one who'd yelled—seemingly came out of a trance. She looked around and realized the position she'd just placed Anna in. The instant self-awareness fell heavily on her, and she couldn't stop apologizing to Anna.

Anna joked about it and assured her it was okay. This kind of thing happened.

\* \* \*

She describes it as a wallop in the face.

On another night, a friend of Anna's who works in the movie industry had a birthday party at a local brewery. They'd known one another for a long time, and because his films showed he had an open-mindedness to darker subject matter, Anna felt comfortable telling him about our family.

When I met him years later at the annual harvest festival, he was very sweet. "You're Anna's mom!" he said with warmth. "I've heard so much about you."

On the night of his fortieth birthday party, the celebration had been going on for a while by the time Anna arrived. She had just stepped through the door, hadn't even taken off her coat, when he excitedly nudged an out-of-town guest and pointed to Anna. Perhaps the beers being served freely by the brewery staff had caused him not to notice how loudly he was speaking when he shouted excitedly over the crowd,

"Dude, this is Bundy's cousin!"

When she told me the story, Anna laughed and did a wonderful impersonation of the way he said it. That awe verging on reverence. "Bundy" could have easily been substituted with "Mick Jagger."

Anna and I talk a lot about this, how strange it is to have a sort of celebrity forced on us for a relationship that we try so hard to hide.

The thing is, I think I get the interest. I believe it's natural. If someone told me they were the cousin of, say, Princess Diana, I'd have the same response. It's like a portal opens to a world people have never been allowed to go into before. They want access to something they find fascinating.

In Anna's stories—and she has many more—they're always good people, well-meaning friends who momentarily lose themselves. Genuine excitement takes over, like a high.

Then, inevitably, they fall back to earth. Their eyes widen, and they look around to see how many people witnessed their brief break with reality. In one case, Anna says another friend literally clapped her hands over her own mouth.

Anna has always had a good sense of humor about it. But she admits she finds this initial loss of control a little troubling. I think she's right. Even now, fifty years later, Ted still has power over people. And it feels a little too much like the power he had when he was still alive, the power he knew how to abuse to manipulate other good, well-meaning people.

※ ※ ※

Not long ago, Anna was invited to participate in a team offsite in San Francisco where the leaders at her company would be able to meet the top brass. To prepare, the internal communications director was putting together a presentation for the event, and she sent around an email asking those attending for intriguing bits of trivia about themselves that she could share during her slideshow. "Do you have an interesting skill?" the email asked. "Are you related to anyone famous?"

A couple of Anna's close colleagues on her team, including her direct boss, knew about her relation to Ted, and when they saw the email, they told her she had to submit it. But Anna felt conflicted. She worried about the setting, feeling it might be inappropriate. But her colleagues insisted she was crazy.

Wanting to be a team player, Anna called the communications director herself. She told her she had an interesting piece of trivia, but she worried about sharing it and wanted to run it by her first.

Anna had barely gotten out Ted's name when a shriek sounded from the other end of her phone. "You have to let me use it," the communications director said. In fact, she told Anna, it was so good she'd save it for the very end.

Anna wasn't convinced. Her bosses would be at the offsite—and her bosses' bosses. The CEO of the company would be there. From Anna's past experiences, she knew how things tended to go when this information was divulged in public settings, and it wasn't great.

But something about this felt different. In the past, Anna had been hiding from the truth when it blindsided her. She realized just how tired she'd grown of letting it spin her into the shadows. If she did this, in a way she'd be stepping out, taking charge.

*Fuck it*, was the way she described the moment of decision to me. She told the communications director to go ahead.

\* \* \*

In San Francisco, the session began, and Anna admitted she felt nervous. She looked around at her coworkers, worried that they'd see her differently after they found out.

Her boss, who'd been one to urge her to do it, sat with Anna as the slideshow played on the big screen while the communications director led at the microphone. Sprinkled throughout the presentation, the other bits of trivia popped up. "Guess who's climbed Mount Rainier?" "Guess who loves to do macramé?"

As the slideshow progressed, the dread officially set in. All the other factoids were innocent, banal even. Anna's boss tried to tell her it would be fine, but Anna could hear the worry in her voice.

Finally, the presentation came to its end, and the communications director turned to the crowd with a big smile. "Now, before I let you all go for happy hour, we have one last bit of trivia. And this one's a doozy." She pulled up the final slide and read the words aloud. "Who in here is closely related to an infamous serial killer?"

Total silence fell.

Everyone began looking around at each other, as if they'd be able to tell, as if they'd recognize some murderous gene in the face of their neighbor. Anna ducked her head. Her boss squeezed her hand tight.

*What have I done?* Anna thought. *What if someone in here is related to a victim?* She longed to go back into the shadows. She wondered how she'd ever thought this was a good idea.

The communications director sauntered her way down from the front until she stood right next to Anna seated in her chair. Then, like the wheel on a game show, she pointed. "It's Anna in HR! Anna, do you want to tell them who it is?"

She offered out the microphone. Anna didn't take it. "Nope," Anna said, wincing. "You go ahead."

The communications director happily took back the microphone, relishing the moment that Anna dreaded. "It's...TED BUNDY!"

The whole place, Anna said, went wild.

❋ ❋ ❋

Afterwards, a strange thing happened. As they released the group for happy hour, a few of Anna's colleagues who'd been sitting nearby flanked her. "So," they said, "tell us everything."

But Anna didn't feel that usual smack in the face. Since she'd been the one to instigate the bomb drop, she saw the aftershocks coming. She didn't miss a step.

And she'd learned a few things over the years about people's questions. First, she didn't believe anymore that she owed anybody answers. Truth was, she didn't have them herself.

But she'd also come to understand that most people appreciated the grimness of the subject matter, that after they recovered from the initial shock, they understood that the topic required the right place and the right time.

"Yeah," Anna said, "we'll talk about it sometime. It's kind of a lot."

Her colleagues got the message, and they didn't press for more. Then, standing in the middle of them, Anna didn't feel alone.

❋ ❋ ❋

Later at happy hour, Anna got a lot of passing comments, strangers who recognized her from the presentation as they crossed through the room.

"Oh, it's you," they'd say. "That's cool."

Though balking a bit at the sentiment (for which I can't help but be reminded of my own memory at the Deluxe 2 restaurant on a fateful day with Ted, when a lunch companion ogled him under the same impression) Anna would return their smile. Whether she liked it or not, Ted was a part of her story, but she'd found a way to take control.

So she'd raise her drink in response. "That's me," she'd say.

*Family celebration. Left to right: Louise Bundy, Edna, Johnnie Bundy, Anna.*

*Edna, Anna, and Don.*

# Invincible

All my life, I've walked. Even as a young girl in Longbranch, I'd set out walking through forests and along the beach. A lot of the time I'd walk alone, looking for other kids to play with.

Walking has always been the way I sort things out in my head. It has been, I suppose, my therapy.

When Anna was a teenager, she began to join me. Even when her schedule got busy, she'd continue to be there by my side. Since she's left the house, we still plan times to get together at least once a week, simply to walk.

\* \* \*

About ten years ago, just a little over a week before Don and I were set to move from West Seattle, Anna and I were out walking with her two dogs along the shoreline. Don had taken a kite up to Alki beach, so we pointed ourselves in that direction, planning to say hi and watch him expertly puppeteer the craft in the sky against the setting sun. Don's flown kites since he was a kid when he handmade his own, discovering he could achieve much better results than his friends with their store-bought kites. Sometimes, with the right conditions, he'd get it a mile high, and he often drew a crowd, even earning a nickname, the "Kite Man" of Alki.

As we neared the beach, we could see him up ahead, his silhouette at one end of the string, a vibrant, bobbing kite way up at the other.

My dad had died a few years previously. Dad was the best gift giver, always wrapping his presents with brightly colored ribbons and string.

After he passed away, Don kept ribbons from my father and tied them onto his kite as a sort of tribute. This was what Anna and I watched dancing in the sky, this cheerful little kite a hundred feet in the air, brilliant ribbons flowing. It was a wonderful, happy sight.

There was an onshore breeze that day, not offshore, and it blew the kite inland towards the business district, a touristy little area. This isn't normally a problem for an expert like Don, but what he hadn't realized was that the shiny, reflective ribbons from my father, chosen because they practically sparkled in the light, contained some sort of conductive material.

The breeze drove the kite right toward a power line.

As it so happens, this was the day before Don's sixty-second birthday. For days, he'd been ruminating about how, since sixty-two meant he'd be able to qualify for social security, he probably needed to behave more maturely, to "straighten up and fly right," and get his act together for what lay ahead.

As Anna and I neared the beach, we waved to Don when, up above, one of the flittering ribbons from the kite touched a power line, then it crossed over to hit the one next to it.

Like magic, the ribbon incinerated with a little puff of smoke. The next thing we saw, a fireball had materialized. *Zzzhoop*—the fireball skittered down the powerline to the next block, where it hit a transformer.

*BOOM.* The transformer exploded with a mushroom cloud. The repercussion was so loud, it nearly knocked us off our feet.

Cars slammed on their brakes and swerved cattywampus in the middle of the street. Dogs barked. Windows opened and curious eyes appeared.

As I mentioned, this was a trendy business district. Spud's, a very popular fish and chips restaurant, sat directly across the street, teeming with customers on this summer evening. All of a sudden, the electricity at Spud's zapped off.

Instantly the business next to it also went dark, and then the one next to that. One after another, all the businesses, restaurants, and apartment buildings along Alki beach lost power.

From our vantage point, Anna and I watched the fallout escalate, stunned. Then—because what else could we do—we began to laugh, uncomfortable gasps tinged with guilt and anxiety. *What had we done? Was this really happening?*

Frantically, Don reeled in his kite. "Get out of here," he called out to us. "Now!"

He was thinking of the time he'd witnessed a coworker, who'd forgotten he had a tall load on the back of his work truck, accidentally take down a power line in front of his company office. When the utility company came out to do a repair, they determined that the driver was at fault and handed his boss a bill for $40,000.

It was with that number going through his head that Don got his kite packed up, and while Anna and I took off in one direction, he headed straight for his van.

Anna and I had a couple of miles to go to get back to her house. As we walked—laughing, our pace a little quicker than usual—we passed by people who saw us coming from the direction of the beach. "Did you see what happened?" they asked. "I heard some guy was flying his kite. I think he hit a power line." Anna and I played dumb, not about to rat out Don, and just kept moving. By the time we reached her house, we were in hysterics.

As we climbed the path up to her front door, her neighbor leaned over from his deck. The strangest thing just happened, he told us. The lights in his house began going off and on, off and on, until everything finally went down. By then, we were a couple miles away from the scene of the crime. "Oh, yeah?" we said, smiling and cringing at the same time. "Hmm, that is strange." Then we ducked into the house and absolutely lost it.

The next thing we knew, a swarm of city light trucks sped by toward the beach, off to replace the transformer and quickly restore power.

Ten days later—days during which Don scrupulously avoided the beach—we moved out of Seattle as previously planned. We never heard about the incident again. Don, the Kite Man of Alki, had had his final hurrah before he turned sixty-two—and we jokingly laughed that he "blew up" Alki Beach.

❊ ❊ ❊

These are not strolls, my walks with Anna. We move vigorously, up hills and down, from sea level ascending to several hundred feet. We often go down to the water, and it's important we stay attuned to the tides so we don't risk getting caught.

When we walk, we're like two limbs of the same organism. So familiar with one another's rhythms and pace, we move seamlessly to single file when the path narrows or steepens, then back in step, side by side, without a word.

I love it when we pass other walkers and joggers, women especially, fellow explorers out taking on the world just like us. I love to know we share this joy.

Then, more and more, I see the tell-tale audio buds glinting in their ears, or the headphones worn like a fashion accessory, blocking out all sound. When we come upon them, I often say hello only to catch them jump, startled by our presence.

Anna's heard me gripe a million times. "They're advertising to the world that they aren't paying attention," I say.

I worry about what might happen to them, the threats they couldn't hear until too late. I can't help it. There are people, I know, who take advantage.

"They think they're invincible," I say. "But they need to be careful."

*Trust, but don't be deceived.* My old mantra.

* * *

What's interesting about walking is that it means Anna and I are facing forward. Every once in a while, we'll turn to look at the other, but most of the time we have to look ahead or risk tripping over our feet.

This arrangement makes it ideal for talking.

By doing away with the necessity of eye contact, we're free to say whatever is on our minds. I suppose that's the reason why confessional boxes in churches keep a separation. I suppose, in a way, that's what Anna's and my walks have become.

When we walk, everything comes out. While one of us speaks, the other listens. We don't have to ask. There is an understanding between us. We are safe.

As such, my daughter and I have gotten to know one another in a way that transcends beyond a shared home and shared name. We know the minutiae of one another's adult lives.

We are, simply put, friends.

Even still, during all our countless walks for almost thirty years, over thousands upon thousands of miles, I never brought up Ted.

* * *

When COVID-19 hit, we—like everyone else—found ourselves dealing with issues we'd never had to deal with, at least not in our lifetimes. As a history major, I'd read a lot about plagues, the way they decimated populations. My mother was born in 1919, just one year after the deadly influenza of 1918 infected more than a third of the world's population. My dad's father had lost most of his siblings to illnesses for which we have vaccinations today. It seemed unreal that we, our modern world, could be dealing with that same type of threat now.

As time went on, the isolation and fear compounded. Every headline, every phone call brought new worries and tragedies. I lost friends and relatives to the disease, and each day I found myself wondering if I'd survive to see the next sunrise.

I couldn't help but wonder, what would go with me when I left?

Anna and I walked a lot during this time, and it was during one of those walks that I inched open the door.

"I feel like I need to talk about Ted," I said.

We were on a road by her house, one we hadn't walked before, but that day we thought we'd try a new direction. We continued a few more steps before Anna answered.

"Is that right?"

I realize now how shocked she was. To have me bring up the subject was downright unheard of. Looking back, I'm impressed she was able to stay composed.

"I feel like I need to get it out of me." I went on. "It's been festering for a while, building and building and building."

I vividly remember the first time I saw the movie *Alien*. When it came out, I was still a young mother at the time, and we'd had to rent not only the video but also the VCR to be able to play it at home. I remember I had to leave the room and watch—peeking from around the corner— during the scene when the creature bursts out of an astronaut's chest.

That scene is the best way I can describe how I felt, urgently, about Ted. I'd repressed my story with painstaking vigilance for most of my life, but suddenly I had to get it out. I had to get it out before it ripped open my rib cage.

In a lot of ways, it reminded me of how I felt right before Ted's execution, when I cold-called Dick Larsen at the *Seattle Times*. I'd felt the primal need to share my story then, too. With surprise, I discovered the need hadn't gone away, nor had it wilted and died from years of neglect. Somehow, it had gotten bigger.

Yet as I said the words, I looked over to gauge Anna's reaction. I worried about her. No matter how hard I've tried to shelter her, it's a difficult subject for her as well. She's acquired her own baggage due to Ted. I waited for her response.

It took her only a moment. "So, you feel like you need to talk about it," she said, urging me on. She's a very good interviewer, my daughter.

"Yeah," I said. "I feel like I need to write about it, but I don't know how to get started."

"Well," Anna said.

The thing about Anna, she has a knack with people. It's a talent she was born with. When she was four years old, she flew by herself to Arkansas to visit my parents (oh, times were different then). Don and I still laugh about when we picked her up at the airport. As soon as she walked off the plane, she ran over to us. "Mom, Dad, I'd like to introduce you to John." She gestured to a very put-together businessman who'd exited the plane behind her. Apparently they'd been seat mates, and Anna had made a new friend. "John, these are my parents," she said formally. We leapt into an apology, hoping that she hadn't bothered him too much, but he waved it off. He assured us Anna had kept him delighted and entertained. She even helped remind him how to solve some math problems. She was four.

But that's Anna. Perhaps some of this is due to her being an only child, but she's always been a connector of people. She collects friends and puts them together. She makes things happen. As a recruiter, she's found a way to do this for a living.

That day as we walked a few more steps down this new road, side by side, eyes pointed forward, I knew she had her reservations about what I'd said. Of course she did. I did, too.

But she laid her reservations aside and put my needs first. Maybe somehow she also sensed it was time.

"Let me talk to some people," Anna said.

* * *

Not long after, I dreamt about Ted.

In the dream, we were kids again, exploring the shore near our family's old cabin in Longbranch. Everything was just as I remembered. Beams of sunlight streamed through the trees and turned to glitter on the surface of the water, which we splashed through, running and laughing.

But even in my merriment, I sensed it. The tide was coming.

As we played, Ted seemed to be searching for something with determination. John and I had no idea what he sought, but we helped look anyway, curious at his purpose.

Soon we gleaned from Ted that he was looking for a "stone." What kind of stone, we didn't know. From where we stood, we could see many stones. Would any do? We very much wanted to help. As we searched, we dodged the waves crashing farther and farther up the shore. Time was running out.

It was my brother who finally put it together. "It's his gravestone," John said, and I instantly knew, with that dream-like certainty, that John was right.

In my dream, Ted was searching for his grave, and I couldn't rest until I led him to it.

* * *

I haven't dreamt about him since.

*Young Edna with brother John (right) at Longbranch.*

# Acknowledgments

First and foremost, the authors wish to acknowledge the women whose own stories were cut short by Ted. The tragedy of each and every life he took cannot be overemphasized.

Along with them, so many other lives were and continue to be impacted by Ted's actions. While writing this book, even more stories have come to our attention. To those who carry the wounds, please know you're not alone.

Many people have been integral in the creation of this book. Together, the authors would like to thank:

Alex Novak, editor and answerer of countless questions. You took a risk on us. Thank you for giving us the chance to tell this story our way.

Sara Ann Alexander, whose editing prowess we only wish we could utilize in all aspects of our lives. Can we keep you, please?

Caitlin DiMotta. Your legal knowledge is matched only by your coolness. We sleep better having you around.

Gwen Nappi. The moment you joined the team, you became family. Now we don't know what we'd do without you.

Steph Marshall, without whom none of this would have happened. You've given us the greatest gift—opportunity—along with your continued support and friendship. Let's meet again in Paris.

Edna would like to thank:

Donald, who has been by my side for over fifty years. He read every page of the manuscript multiple times contributing valuable insights, stories, and observations. All our years together, even during the toughest times, he managed to make me laugh.

My daughter, Anna. Without her connections none of this would have been possible. From the very beginning her wise counsel and unconditional support carried me forward.

My grandson, N.C., for all the joy he brings us.

My brother, John, for bravely sharing his stories and calling me frequently to cheer me on.

My dear friends and relatives for generously providing encouragement when they knew this was a tough subject for me to confront. Some of them appear in the book, and I'm grateful for being able to share their stories. Special thanks to—Mary, Ann, John, Larry, Tom, Bruce, Steve, Scott, Jeanie, Margie, Pamela, Annie, Marsha, Oona, Blair & Amelia, Lee, Karla, Millie, Rich & Maureen, Gary, Mike & Judy, Fiori & Maryanna.

Megan would like to thank:

Laraine and Hal, my day-one constants. No matter how turned around I get, I always know you have my back.

Shane, my co-conspirator, my touchstone, my cheerleader, and my secret weapon. Like the card said, 'til death do us part is for quitters.